THE

Mississippi Quarterly

SERIES IN SOUTHERN LITERATURE

THE

Mississippi Quarterly

SERIES IN SOUTHERN LITERATURE

under the general editorship of

PEYTON W. WILLIAMS

THE FORM DISCOVERED

Essays on the Achievement of Andrew Lytle

M. E. BRADFORD, EDITOR

THE FORM DISCOVERED

THE FORM DISCOVERED

Essays on the Achievement of
ANDREW LYTLE

EDITED BY M. E. BRADFORD

PUBLISHED FOR THE *MISSISSIPPI QUARTERLY* BY THE
UNIVERSITY AND COLLEGE PRESS OF MISSISSIPPI

JACKSON

The essays by Thomas H. Landess, Madison Jones, Charles
C. Clark, H. L. Weatherby, Edward Krickel, M. E. Brad-
ford, and Sidney J. Landman, and the checklist by Noel
Polk, appeared previously in the *Mississippi Quarterly*, 23
(Fall 1970).

The essay "The Local Universality of Andrew Lytle"
appeared previously as the "Foreword" to *The Hero with
the Private Parts* (Baton Rouge, 1966) and is reprinted
with the permission of the Louisiana State University
Press.

The essay "Yankees of the Race: The Decline and Fall
of Hernando de Soto," by Robert G. Benson, appeared
previously in a different form under another title in *The
Georgia Review*, 27 (Summer 1973), and is reprinted with
permission of that journal.

THIS VOLUME IS AUTHORIZED
AND SPONSORED BY
MISSISSIPPI STATE UNIVERSITY
MISSISSIPPI STATE, MISSISSIPPI

Contents

The
Mississippi Quarterly
Series
in Southern Literature

Mississippi Quarterly: The Journal of Southern Culture, as its title implies, is an interdisciplinary journal dealing with all aspects of the life and civilization of the American South; it is now in its twenty-sixth year of publication under the sponsorship of Mississippi State University. For many years, and with increasing distinction, the *Quarterly* has given major attention to Southern writers of all periods by publishing critical and scholarly articles, bibliographies, edited source materials, letters and reviews; by sponsoring symposia; and by publishing numerous special issues each concerned with the work of a single Southern author. This year, in conjunction with Mississippi State University and the University and College Press of Mississippi, it is initiating a series of volumes to be designated The *Mississippi Quarterly* Series in Southern Literature, of which *The Form Discovered* is the first. A collection on William Faulkner, now in press, will be the first in a sub-series on Faulkner to appear at frequent intervals during the next several years. A second sub-series will consist of bibliographical studies, and the general series is intended to include editions of significant source materials for the study of Southern letters as well as further general critical and scholarly works.

That Other Eden in the West:
A Preface to Andrew Lytle

M. E. BRADFORD

SOMETIME IN THE coming year we should see the publication of Andrew Lytle's long awaited memoir. He has called it *A Wake for the Living*. And the entitling was not casually intended. For Mr. Lytle has seen a good bit of history and has reflected on a great deal more. And it is the history of European man in this hemisphere which has been his reiterative subject: more particularly, the history of what this ambitious extension of the West has signified to the millions drawn to play a part in it by a very special set of expectations.

The burden of Lytle's narratives has been that this adventure has not, on the whole, gone well. We, the heirs of this legion of émigrés are, we tell ourselves, alive and full of possibilities; but it is also, we recognize, a tenuous sort of existence which we retain—so tenuous that, in its common features, we can recognize the occasion for rites funereal, a valediction to the disposition of things which contained and supported our generic humanity during the past two and one-half millennia. Mr. Lytle agrees with Aristotle that man is a social creature, not to be defined or understood outside the context of an established civilization. And he further agrees with many classical and most Christian political and social philosophers that civilization (or the Commonweal) has great difficulty in restraining the perversities of the human will and spirit: that is, unless it enjoys some tangency and reinforcement with and from the more inclusive ordering of creation which is its original (i.e., as a Godsweal). In brief, it requires a religious ground. Otherwise, those lies with which the Enemy has always beguiled us will, in our delusion that we made (or can make) ourselves, collapse the frail supports which shore up the walls of the city. In the opening lines of the first published section of *A Wake for the Living* Lytle announces as his purpose "to tell my girls who they are." By being faithful to this objective he is, however, addressing a far larger audience—Southern and American—and finally including all that was Christendom. And this is what he has been doing all the time.

But I must be specific. Once believed, the "great lie" which drew our European forefathers to a "new world" becomes a geographical variant of the oldest mortal error, the expectancy of some easy and un-earned improvement in their contingent status, only this time by means of relocation: a place, not an apple. R. W. B. Lewis, David W. Noble, Leo Marx, and Ernest Lee Tuveson have examined the American evi-dence which demonstrates the wide distribution of this dream of a "new" or "other" Eden. As private objective we speak of it as "the pursuit of happiness"—according to Mr. Lytle "the most hopelessly delusive of all" the characteristic American notions. In its personal or collective form, it is now the governing preoccupation of scholarship on our native literature. And it has a bearing on this study.

The notion that life on this side of the Atlantic carries with it some automatic exemption from the consequences of the Fall is implicit in much of Lytle's fiction, examined there "in the flesh." It is sounded in his "Introduction" to the second edition of his life of Nathan Bedford Forrest. And it is recurrent in his criticism. *That idea, or its immediate and terrible consequences in the worship of those minions of the arch-fiend: Power, Mass, and Speed!* I refer the reader to his masterful papers on Faulkner, to the matter of the Garden in *The Velvet Horn*, to the tales of Spanish conquest, and even to the motives driving Henry Brent in his restoration of *The Grove* in *A Name For Evil*. The com-mentary gathered in this volume (all written before the composition of its preface) offers further attestation of this connection between Lytle and the work of his countrymen. But it is, of course, generally a negative conjunction. For, in Lytle's own words, "the westward movement of Europeans, beginning with Columbus, not only shattered the narrow physical boundaries of Christendom but . . . [also] weak-ened it by reducing a union composite of spiritual and temporal parts to the predominance of material ends." In other words, a dark spirit and a wicked will have had from its inception a hand in our journey. And we are, in the course of five centuries, proven to be incapable of recognizing their presence until the damage is done.

A Wake for the Living is, of course, a personal document. The fortune of Mr. Lytle's kindred, their friends, neighbors, and antagonists, and the larger envelope of movements and events brought to focus in these individual lives—all standing just behind the life of the speaker—give dramatic force, concreteness, and purchase to his exploration of a private past. History is most visible *and* available in their lineaments. They remind us of the high value attached to a genuine identity in a world where *no one* is *anyone*. For such identity is among the casualties of habitation in a false paradise: apart from great peril to the immortal soul, perhaps the most serious casualty. And to live among "nobodies" is almost the same as living among the dead—the equivalent of a wake. Or perhaps it is even worse than a wake. That ceremony belongs to families living in places (the former being impossible without the latter). And both of these necessary props to identity are now much desiccated by two other demons, Mobility and Equality. Mr. Lytle's reminiscences recall what was lost by telling his reader of *a* family in *a* place. In their particularity they bring home to us the price of such a loss. The merit of his narrative will be, at least in part, the richness and variety of the life it contains—its multiplicity of aside, anecdote, and digression. These diversities are integral to its thrust. They spell out how personhood with the irreducible complexities it engenders, and not some remote Zeitgeist, makes for history. And how that sans such interwoven histories *qua* history there is nothing for the artist to tell.

But there is another observation I must make about *A Wake for the Living*, lest I misdirect its future readers. Every page of the book reminds us that, as substitute Edens go, Middle Tennessee (its setting) stood up rather well. Even in his darkest moments, Lytle offers little to the contrary. Renaissance and post-Renaissance Europeans stand on one side of his affirmation of that place and that fact, the American Indian on the other. Yet there is no evidence of mere sentiment in anything Lytle has composed about his *patria*. Indeed, the Tennessee of his fathers is in its characteristic manifestations saluted with elegiac affirmation chiefly because it never seriously imagined itself an Eden—because the South always understood that it could be no more than an extension and perhaps a very modest improvement of and upon an older England, not the Zion or the "new" Jerusalem of the eschatologists. In so far as its ambitions were modest and "worldly," the region continued a civil polity. For its ends were not mislabelled or glorified. And this made a considerable difference, despite private and individual moments of participation in the larger American myth, and despite a deficient theology. Said another way, *A Wake for the Living*, rooted in the full experience of his life, should be useful as a gloss on everything Andrew Lytle has written. Along with his essays in opinion, it will—if employed with care and with regard to the special imperatives of criticism or fiction—point toward fruitful lines of inquiry in both of these connections. And as I insisted above, the book will also reaffirm the intellectual unity of Lytle's total achievement, the oneness of his song.

The producers of the papers gathered in this collection have provided the occasion for these prefatory remarks. Their focus is appropriately upon Lytle's fiction; and in the process of tending to their explicatory business they have impressed their editor with the functional interaction of their observations. For the careful reader of Mr. Lytle, these essays come together. They deliver to him the artist at work, in the process of discovering the proportions of something both ancient and perpetually new in the matter under pressure from the forming imagination. Here past is present in what Lytle calls "the peculiar possibility of fiction," here the "author's seeing eye" is penetrated and reproduced in the necessary sacrilege of critical exposition. Also it is to be hoped that the novelist's effort to "create his reader as well as [his] book" has been furthered in days and situations to come by the readings he has helped to create in these pages.

The emphasis of this volume has the shortcomings of the Fall 1970 issue of *Mississippi Quarterly* from which it is largely drawn: a neglect of Lytle the critic and Lytle the historian or social observer. Likewise, in due course, more should be said of his poetics, of his large view of the craft of fiction. But for this first overview of his career it was agreed by all the hands joined in that labor that the first priority would have to go to the novels and short stories. Our hope is to stimulate interest in that making, to call for much needed republication. For Lytle has been, in our century, one of the masters of his art. And this part of his achievement has an indisputable right to the attention offered here. That attention, and more!

THE FORM DISCOVERED

Unity of Action in *The Velvet Horn*

THOMAS H. LANDESS

CAROLINE GORDON, a critic whose literary instincts have always been remarkably reliable, has said of *The Velvet Horn*: "I suspect that it is a landmark in American fiction. I do not know of any novel like it." Surely she must be right about its greatness and its originality; and these qualities derive in large measure from the awesome complexity of the work which allows the author to give free rein to his technical virtuosity while ranging over a subject which is as vast and imposing as any explored in modern fiction. After finishing *The Velvet Horn* the reader is overwhelmed by the sheer scope of experience and sensibility which went into the making of the novel, in the same way that he is overwhelmed after reading the works of Dostoevsky or Faulkner (but not the works of, say, Hemingway, whose range of experience is well within the imagination of the average college student).

One has to admire the total achievement of the work: the broad spectrum of characters, the variety of incident, the beautifully cut details, the shifting levels of language. But inevitably the very richness of structure and texture poses a problem in unity which has proven the undoing of more than one reader. Here, as with *Ulysses*, the novice is likely to quit early rather than to make that first synthesis which gives him all he needs to continue until the end. And with both novels, in order to make this synthesis it is almost necessary first to grasp the essential heart of the work, the archetypal or universal experience which lies at the core of the action—or, as Mr. Lytle would insist, envelops it.

When one discusses unity of action in *The Velvet Horn*, then, it is finally the archetypal action that defines the thematic terms in which the dramatic action must be understood. And it is a failure to understand the true nature of this archetypal experience in all of its manifestations which has led some readers mistakenly to conclude that there are several dramatic actions which are linked thematically—the usual structure in novels of complexity—rather than one important archetypal action which is stated and restated in a variety of contexts during the course of the novel. Once this distinction is understood, then the true significance and originality of the work emerge with striking clarity.

I

Before a detailed examination of the novel, therefore, it is perhaps necessary to clarify the function of the archetypal action in fiction and to ascertain its nature and operation in *The Velvet Horn*. To begin with, in any literary work of lasting significance the experience we call archetypal creates *in potentia* its own implicit form, a paradigm which molds or receives the structure and texture of a novel even as it is put together by the artist. The paradigm is simple but constant and finds its most obvious definition in myth, which purifies significant human experience and is, for this reason, forever preserved in the racial memory, both at the conscious and the unconscious levels. Myth often guides the literary artist in working out his own rendition of the action or experience; and symbol embodies or epitomizes its essence; but it is finally the paradigm itself which in the genuine masterpiece generates all of these devices and keeps the writer true to what is permanent in man's nature.

The archetypal experience which Mr. Lytle explores in *The Velvet Horn* can best be defined in theological terms, though many other definitions are possible. It is in essence nothing less than the fall of man from a state of innocence, his suffering as a consequence, and his redemption, partially through grace, which leads finally to reintegration into the order of things. The myth which best exemplifies this experience is, of course, the Garden of Eden story: but there have been other more complex renditions, something more than myth, which after all has its esthetic limitations. *The Divine Comedy* is certainly one example of a more sophisticated statement and Milton's *Paradise Lost* is another. In more modern times some of the novels of Faulkner come to mind. This, then, is the true subject of *The Velvet Horn*; and the paradigm which preceded by implication its creation is the same one which surely controlled the ordering of these other great works.

Though I have mentioned examples which are Christian, since Mr. Lytle uses the same traditional mythology as Dante and Milton, there are certainly myths in other cultures which are identical in their essential nature and of which Mr. Lytle is obviously aware. For example, almost every traditional society ritualizes the experience of lost innocence in an initiation ceremony which introduces the young man or young woman into the dangers and difficulties of the life struggle, as well as clarifies the social and moral significance of sexuality—that is, defines for each the primary role that he or she will play in society. In primitive tribes the young man may be exposed to danger and even physical torture, while the young woman is ceremonially deflowered, in some societies actually so. In more highly developed cultures, however, such rituals are more often symbolic: the boy is introduced into the ritual of the hunt and the girl makes her debut. After these "ceremonies" they are accepted into the adult community: the young man is a full-fledged hunter, and the young woman is ready to receive serious callers.

The Christian myth, of course, elevates this primitive ritual to a cosmic significance and explains in theological terms each of the stages in the initiation. Thus childhood is the Garden of Eden, free from knowledge, which must come inevitably through contact with evil. In the Christian myth the consequences of such evil are pain and death, while in the primitive ritual these are almost always the evil itself. The promise of Heaven which comes through Christ's pain and death is roughly equivalent to the acceptance of the youth into the adult community, after pain and death have been endured or risked and, by implication, conquered, at least in the province of the heart. In the Christian myth, of course, Christ suffers for all men what each primitive youth had to suffer for himself, but it is just as true that all Christians, through the acceptance of the faith, must repeat that sacrifice over and over again, not only in such rituals as the mass, but also in their daily lives.

There are, however, other ways of looking at the relationship between the initiation ceremony and the myth of the Garden: the former exists in time and the latter encompasses all of time; the former is specific and the latter is generic; one is the effect, the other the cause. Thus, the individual in the ritual of initiation must face pain and death at a moment in time because at the beginning of time his primal parents lost their innocence and in doing so necessitated the subsequent loss of his. Eden, then, is the story of the family of man, and the initiation ceremony celebrates the acceptance, after suffering, of one individual into the full responsibility of that family.

Once the essential unity of these two actions, whether mythic or ritualistic, is understood, then the paradigmatic unity of *The Velvet Horn* is apparent, and the several courses of action are seen to be essentially the same action.

II

Let us now examine the action of the novel in the light of the archetypal paradigm which shaped it. The three most important characters are the boy, Lucius Cree, his mother, Julia, and his uncle, Jack Cropleigh; and each of these is involved in a separate formulation of the archetype; though these plot lines intersect at certain important dramatic junctures, it is their apparent discretion, seemingly absolute to some readers, which needs explanation. Like Milton, Lytle begins his version of the Eden myth *in medias res* with the novice Lucius Cree as his focal character. Time present, then, can be defined as "after the fall," when the young man begins to learn the hard lessons of manhood and to feel for the first time the consequences of his family heritage— which, as in all families, is one of sin and shame. The initial action seems almost irrelevant to what follows. In Part One, entitled "The Peaks of Laurel," Lucius and his uncle Jack climb a mountain to "witch a well" for some neighbors; and in the course of this adventure, young Cree is seduced by the mountain folk, who seem on the surface to be looser in their moral conduct than his own family. At the end of the long section, Lucius learns that the man he supposes to be his father, Captain Cree, has been killed by a falling tree. Thus we see the beginnings of an initiation story and are prepared for another Southern *bildungsroman*. But at the beginning of Part Two, "The Water Witch," the young man and his uncle start back to the valley; and at this stage the narrative shifts its focus to Jack Cropleigh, the garrulous and introspective uncle, who recalls earlier years and the flight into the woods of his sister, Julia (Lucius' mother), with Pete Legrand, where they are pursued by the girl's brothers, apprehended and punished: Legrand is disemboweled and Julia is summarily married to her upright cousin Joe Cree. As Jack's character develops, he reveals himself more and more as a prophet, one who knows and suffers the sins of his own blood. And in juxtaposing this section with the first, Mr. Lytle is able to define the essential thematic structure of the novel—the relationship between the initiation of Lucius and the Christ-like role of Jack Cropleigh.

III

As in any good work of fiction, all structural and textural devices serve to further the thematic intent, and at the outset Lytle introduces two dominant symbols which themselves embody the meaning of the narrative and unite the two ostensibly different experiences in one image. These symbols are the "velvet horn" and the tree; and Lytle, in his essay "The Novelist and the Mythmaking Process," himself clarifies the meaning of the former, as follows:

> Where symbols appear—and there will be one to contain them all in their relationships—they represent the entire action by compressing into a sharp image or succession of images the essence of meaning. For example, in animal nature, the horn stands for both the masculine and feminine parts of being, the two aspects of the apposites which make a whole: the two in one contained by a single form. Add the velvet to this and you posit the state of innocence, that suspension before the act which continues the cycle of creation. At a certain moment the buck, out of the mystery of instinct, rubs the velvet off against the tree, and then he is ready for the rutting season. The velvet grows about the feminine end of the horn, and it bleeds as it is rubbed away. The blood is real, but the act symbolizes what the other end of the horn will do. In human nature the horn's counterpart would be the hermaphrodite, Hermes and Aphrodite contained within the one form. Their separation, Eve taken from Adam's side, at another level continues the cycle of creation. Both forms exist within the constancy of the seasonal turn of nature. The entire range of imagery relates to these.

Lytle feels that this is the "controlling image" of the novel; but the tree, I would suggest (admittedly with some presumption), is the more dominant and pervasive of the two. For one thing, it links thematically the myth of the Garden with the initiation ceremony and thereby suggests the unity of all action in the novel. (The horn performs the same function, but does so only after one understands the brilliant but highly specialized literary function of sexuality which Mr. Lytle has defined in his essay.) The tree which falls on Joe Cree in the prologue to the first section is of course the archetypal tree of knowledge: Cree has discovered that Lucius is not his son but the product of Julia's illicit conduct prior to marriage. This discovery is too much for the proud man to bear; and so, in an act perfectly symbolic, he commits suicide, destroyed by his own new understanding of an old sin.

But the tree also reminds one of the ancient rites of initiation, when the young candidate was sent into the woods to brave danger, armed often enough with only a primitive weapon emblematic of his essential innocence. So does Lucius Cree go into the woods with his uncle to witch the well, just as his mother "went into the woods," first with her brother Duncan and later with Pete Legrand. As a matter of fact, to point up the important correspondence between the actions of both generations, Lucius' first sexual experience, with the low-born Ada Rutter, occurs within sight of the place where his mother lost her virginity in an incestuous union with Duncan. Thus, the forest (in this case Parcher's Cove, the obvious equivalent of Eden) provides the perfect setting for sin—both the original and the inevitable re-enactment. And the tree, in its traditional as well as its contextual meaning, is the perfect image to bind the Christian myth and the pagan rite into a viable unity.

In addition to the tree, there are other symbols which work toward the same end. For example, the mountain in the first section recalls not only Dante's purgatory, the categories of sin which every Christian must surmount, but also the hardship of primitive exposure which here has a counterpart in the struggle of Lucius to comprehend the meaning of his encounter with the harsh facts of human existence: the filth in which the mountain men live; their lust, which causes Lucius' young friend Jeff to battle his own father; the easy virtue of the mountain women. From a horrified bystander, Lucius is transformed into an active participant when he forces himself on the willing Ada Belle in order to assert his sense of manhood, which has been aroused by the conduct of those around him.

Water is likewise an important symbol. The mountainfolk lack water, and it is for this reason that Jack and Lucius are on the mountain in the first place, Jack as "the water witch" who can find the best spot for a well by using his own intuition and a divining rod. And it is in this activity that the reader sees the first hint of Jack's thematic function in the novel—that of prophet-redeemer, the Christ figure in the action. For water in its Christian ceremonial use is redemptive, the element symbolic of God's greatest gift to mankind—Christ's sacrifice, the benefit of which man receives in the first sacrament, when he is baptized into the efficacy of the crucifixion and is "resurrected" or given second life as one initiated into the communion of the faithful. Baptism, then, is the Christian equivalent of the pagan initiation rite—and water is another significant symbol linking Christian tradition with the more primitive ceremonies.

Jack Cropleigh, then, is the man whose special province is water; and as he is able to find the well on the mountain in the earlier sections of the novel, so in the end is he able to redeem Lucius and transform the young man's illicit relationship with Ada Belle into a beautiful and satisfying marriage. Here the link with Christian mythology is unmistakable; Jack makes the sexual fall of Lucius ultimately "fortunate" by sanctifying the marriage with his blood. As Jack intervenes to protect Lucius from the logical consequences of his act, namely, death at the hands of Ada Belle's outraged brother, so Christ redeemed the children of Adam from the consequences of original sin which logically led to damnation, or eternal separation from God. And Lytle makes it quite clear in his own discussion of the book that the union of lovers, the rejoining of the male and the female in the sexual act, is the symbolic equivalent of regaining, within the framework of the human condition, the innocence and wholeness of the Garden prior to the fall.

In addition to symbols, Lytle employs the device of a special point of view to reinforce and clarify the unity of action. As a result of his redemptive role in the fictional drama, Jack Cropleigh emerges as the central character. In his consciousness both the eternal myth of the Garden (the story of Julia, Duncan, and their incestuous union in Parcher's Cove) and the ritual of the initiation (the struggle in time present of Lucius Cree to achieve manhood and wholeness) are perfectly contained, since Jack is the only witness to both actions and has the remarkable capacity to live in imagination the lives of others as if they were his own. Lytle calls Jack the "spiritual hermaphrodite," suggesting the ancient myth of Teiresias, who, being both male and female, was able to know all experience. As Lytle says of Jack:

> He alone could suffer the entire myth . . . . Having set him apart with no life of his own, other than his entanglement with all life viewed by family and community, he was best suited to control as central intelligence, and his office as victim-savior could bring it all to a focus by his death.

Thus, the point of view shifts from Lucius as soon as the boy learns of Joe Cree's death, or, as soon as the family's earlier sins begin to weigh on his shoulders; and from that time forward, though the focus often shifts from one character to another, the reader feels that these shifts are not entirely away from Jack, but are in some sense his "translations" of the experience of others: hence one is able to reside, for a time, even, in the consciousness of the dead Duncan, who, without such a device, could only be a ghostly wraith of the past rather than the palpable character-in-action so essential to good fiction.

Thus this subtle, and as far as I can tell, original juxtaposition of time past and time present in the consciousness of just such a character is yet another way in which the author reinforces the essential unity of all the seemingly separate actions. Just as the paradigms underlying both the Garden myth and the initiation ceremony are ultimately the same paradigm, just as the symbols of the tree, the mountain, and water function to unite these paradigms, so does Jack, who participates fully in both the eternal past and the temporal present, function as a unifying force in the novel.

At first, of course, the unity of the separate actions is not apparent, since Lytle does not pursue his narrative in chronological or even logical order. In this respect the analogy between the beginning of *The Velvet Horn* and *Paradise Lost* breaks down after the initial switch from time present to time past, for Milton's structure is essentially artificial, in deference to a classical tradition: but Lytle's action in *The Velvet Horn* is ordered according to the structure of the mind, the human consciousness, and it is in Jack Cropleigh that this structure has its ultimate authority. Without this unifying character, the novelist would have been forced into discursive segments in order to define the relationship between the various parts of his sequential narrative. As it stands, the mere juxtaposition of events, past and present, in the mind of Jack Cropleigh serves to point up their thematic relationship. Thus in Section Two, called "The Water Witch," where all the significant conflicts and relationships are defined, Jack relives part of Julia's story (the incident with Pete Legrand) only to return to the present, where Lucius is blaming himself for Joe Cree's death.

> They drove a little way when Lucius spoke harshly.
> "It's my fault," he said.
> "Hush, boy. Hush," Jack said, startled.
> "When I did it up there with that girl, I knew something bad would happen."

Cree's suicide, of course, is the direct result of his knowledge about the earlier indiscretion of Julia and Pete, the event Jack has been reliving at the moment Lucius interrupts his reverie. But the young man's feeling of guilt is not without validity, for in his moment of initiation into knowledge of adult sexuality, he has without knowing it almost perfectly reenacted the sin of his mother; and thus, in a very real sense, he does share in the death of Joe Cree, who kills himself because he knows that Lucius is not his son. With the eye of omniscience Jack Cropleigh recognizes the intrinsic relationship of the two actions in the closing pages of Part Two.

> "God, is there only one image of fatality? Put Pete Legrand in the place of this boy Jeff; put Julia in her son's place. Find nineteen lost years and stand Beverly and Duncan and Dickie beside him and it would be the same. No, Duncan was halted by the dead fire. It would be the same, as long as the eyelids stay shut. Out of all the combinations possible is fatality so dull as to find one posture, one only, that self-begetting, self-perpetuating wholeness before division, division which is knowledge, the bitter first fruit whose aftertaste set us slobbering, wanderers in this world?"

IV

Returning to the action, then, after the Cropleigh family history is recreated in "The Water Witch," the narrative in Part Three is again set in time present, but for a while in the consciousness of Pete Legrand, who has heard of Cree's death and, unaware of his own role in it, rides toward Julia's house to renew his courtship after nearly two decades. Once again time past intersects with time present, and the essential structure of Jack Cropleigh's reminiscence while riding along with Lucius is paralleled in "The Passionate Husk" as Legrand relives the past while journeying with a companion toward the Cree house. And though for a part of the novel the reader views the action through the eyes of Pete Legrand and a series of choral characters who live along the road he is riding, there is still a sense in which this segment is merely a repetition of what has already been told, a sharp underlining of the significant unity of all experience.

The fourth section of the novel, entitled "The Wake," is primarily concerned with Lucius' introduction to the reality of death—one of the basic lessons learned in the initiation ceremony; and at one point in the narrative Lytle underscores the importance of this archetype in a speech by Jack to his nephew.

"The Indian boy was always put down among the women, but the time came when they drove a stick through the fleshy part of his chest, tied thongs at each end and from there to the pole, and all day long leaning back to keep the thong tight, with head back and eyes open to the sun, he followed it blazing about the pole. And in the West there are no trees or clouds to block the view. And it may be the pain in his chest eased the pain in his eye, and there were the drums to beat up his courage, and maybe the chanting distracted him some. But if he made the circle, the boy died but the man was there. And afterwards the horizon did not seem the promise or terror of space, nor did he see in the seasons the grind of time but in both that eternal reflection, for he had seen the circle come back on itself, and that great distance the sun come down to the eye, one blinding whiteness, one bright pain—flesh, body, time, space, center, circumference—forever drowned in that illumination which is all. That's why the Indian's eye is clear and steady. It opens at dawn and shuts at night in the afterglow of that mystery."

But Lucius is not the only one who is brought face to face with the knowledge of death. For Jack, initiate though he is, has a special destiny in store for him which he comes to understand during this night given over to communal mourning and reminiscence. After drinking heavily, Jack falls into the grave dug for Joe Cree, and at that moment sees in a prophetic vision the origin of all the troubled action: the incestuous union of Julia and Duncan from which Lucius has come. And it is this experience that prepares him for the role of savior and begins to define for him the necessity of his own sacrifice.

The fifth section, "The Night Sea Journey," is concerned in large measure with a proof of the boy's newly won manhood and the final acting out of Jack's passion. Once again, the seemingly separate actions have the same underlying thematic significance and in the concluding scenes are linked together dramatically. Lucius, now a man in every sense of the word, has assumed the responsibility for Joe Cree's lumber mill, still unaware of his true origins. Here Lytle's preoccupation with the matter of business may seem curious on the surface, though it is amply prepared for in earlier sections. Thematically, however, it is inevitable; for what does a young man do after initiation but take up his masculine responsibilities as provider? In primitive tribes it was the role of hunter that he assumed; in more modern times it is business, farming, or one of the professions to which he addresses himself. And it is absolutely necessary that this facet of the theme be explored, since it is into the realities of the struggle for survival—the necessary condition of all life—that the initiate is introduced. Thus the paradigm demands such conduct of Lucius; and one sees the full measure of Lytle's control of his material in the financial intricacies that surround the cutting and selling of timber— activities which form an integral part of the action in the novel.

It is also significant that once again the image of the tree focuses the eye of the reader on the meaning of the action. The cutting and selling of the timber, after all, is the perfect symbol of man's ability to transform his experience of danger into a viable means of survival. Just as the primitive hunter was able to learn, in his ritual journey into the wilderness, the skills of survival which proved his eventual worth to the tribe, so Lucius, after braving the Peaks of Laurel, is able to cut timber and market it—even able to build a house for himself, Ada Belle, and their coming child out of the very tree which killed Joe

Cree. Thus, in a sense he proves himself a better man than the man who was supposedly his father, because when he discovers the secret of his mother's affair with Pete Legrand, he is able to live with the knowledge, even to build on it, while Joe Cree allows it to destroy him. And fully rendering the symbolic implications of the tree, Lytle once again links initiation to the myth of the Garden—and so fulfills all of the thematic and aesthetic promises made in the opening section.

Jack Cropleigh is similarly changed as a result of his fall into Joe Cree's grave; and, interestingly enough, he too embarks on a financial course of action roughly parallel to Lucius' in order to save Julia and his nephew from the ruin he believes inevitable, a ruin he fears will result in exploitation at the hands of Pete Legrand. A mule breeder by vocation and temperament, Jack becomes an aggressive trader, leaves his farm, and travels through South Alabama and Georgia, like any pitchman. He too begins to assume, for the first time, the full responsibilities of his blood, and thus is transformed from the oft-times drunken philosopher into the man of action. All that is left for him is the final assumption of responsibility, which is the sacrifice of his life for the perpetuation of the family.

This sacrifice comes at the end of the novel, after Lucius has accepted the full consequences of his own manhood by marrying Ada Belle. In a climactic scene the young couple is confronted in Jack's house by both families, Ada's mother and brother Othel on the one hand, and Lucius' mother and uncle on the other. Jack, who is at last satisfied with his nephew's maturity, gives his blessing to the marriage once he fully understands it; and when the retarded Othel raises a gun to shoot Lucius, Jack steps in front of his nephew and takes the blast—the martyred redeemer.

In Jack's death the dispute over Lucius' marriage is ended, and the tragedy brings everyone to a final understanding and acceptance of his own sin. Julia, for example, after Jack has drawn his last breath, turns to Lucius and whispers, "Duncan. Duncan . . . '" an acknowledgement of her guilt, but when Lucius attempts to support her, she tells him, "No, no, . . . your place is with your wife." Lucius likewise feels his complicity in Jack's death, not only because his runaway marriage has been the occasion for the fatal meeting, but also because in order to make his entrance more dramatic, he does not immediately tell the assembled kinsmen that his union with Ada Belle has been legitimatized. And Legrand, who has married Julia and assumed the burden of paternal responsibility for Lucius (even though Julia has told him the truth before their marriage), must also live with the fact that the woman whom he has idealized for so long has suddenly grown old, as if in the moment of Jack's murder the years of guilt had suddently crowded in on her as they inevitably do, ever so slowly, to everyone as a consequence of the first fall. Yet it is Legrand, the "outsider," who puts into words the beneficent consequences of Jack's sacrifice: " 'Jack's death will bring us all together. Your mother mentioned it might be well for your cousin to teach Ada Belle her letters. I think that's a good sign, don't you?' "

And so the family—which in its broadest meaning represents the larger community, the family of mankind—is humbled and reunited, just as man after the fall is first humbled by suffering and death and then redeemed by Christ, whose sacrifice makes possible a reunion in God of all who admit their sins and seek the benefits of that sacrifice. Thus man—initiated into knowledge at the fall—may transcend the consequences of his own initiation through love. And Lytle brings the two into perfect focus, so that their essential unity is clear.

V

It is this unity, I would suggest, which has provoked Miss Gordon's striking endorsement of the novel, and she has by no means exaggerated its intrinsic value. *The Velvet Horn* is surely one of the great literary achievements of the Southern renaissance and one of the most significant novels of the twentieth century. Its marvelous complexity has made it inaccessible to a wide readership; but in time, when the intricacies of design are further clarified by critical commentary, like *Ulysses* it will begin to reach the greater audience it obviously deserves.

A Look at "Mister McGregor"

MADISON JONES

I HAVE LEARNED many things of value from Andrew Lytle, but
now, as I consider again his story "Mister McGregor," one of them
especially stands out in my mind. I learned it in those creative writing
classes of his at the University of Florida; and so did all the rest of his
serious students. Though a hard one at first, it was a simple lesson. It
was simply that fiction writing is work, and strenuous work. Fiction
writing was a craft, an exceptionally difficult craft, and like any other
it had to be mastered. There was more besides involved, to be sure, but
this was locked up in the person, and the only way it could emerge
was through the person's mastery of the craft. And so he taught us
craft. Or, it might be more accurate to say, he taught us the scrupulous
attention to it, since finally a writer can learn his business only in
doing it.

Mr. Lytle told us this and showed it to us in our own work. But he
showed it to us in still another and even more convincing way, if we
read his fiction. For there, from first to last, was an exceptionally vivid
example of a man's practicing what he preached. (Or, as well, preach-
ing what he practiced.) What was clear enough then has been made
still more emphatically clear by publication of *The Velvet Horn*: that
here was a writer whose unsparing attention to his craft had transformed it from merely that into art of a distinguished order. Here was
an art that by precision of language and rendered detail, by alertness
to form and to each new implication of image, not only used but used
up its subject and drew the eye through the particular into the
universal.

I remember, as Mr. Lytle's student, supposing that this consciousness of the necessity for scrupulous craftsmanship was something he
had learned only through the continuous practice of his art. Later,

looking back more seriously at the first of his published fiction, I changed my mind. Then I came to believe, as I still do believe, that this consciousness was a thing he was either born with or else, more probably, derived from the vanished society out of which he came—a consciousness based on the knowledge that we can transcend matter only by means of it. This, in terms of art, implies craftsmanship, and it was something Mr. Lytle seemed to know very perfectly at least from the time of his first published story, "Mister McGregor," in 1935.

"Mister McGregor" is a story that was slow to receive due appreciation, by me as by others. The reason in my own case was simply that for a long time I did not see the ultimate point of the story and so missed the fullness of its power. I did appreciate the dramatic force of its surface action, the fierce and beautifully sustained conflict resulting in the victory of the husband over his wife. But I entirely missed the essential role of the story's narrator and therefore failed to comprehend the tragic implication of the whole.

The narrator of course is all-important, for the story is in fact his own story. At first glance, however, his role seems merely secondary, the agency by which an appalling battle of the sexes is dramatically related to the reader. Mister McGregor, the master of a plantation in slave times, against accepted usage and over the bitter protest of his strong-willed wife, whips his wife's personal female slave for her blatant impudence. In consequence the slave woman's husband, a proud and dangerous Negro who is humiliated beyond all bounds by the punishment of his wife, makes up his mind to get vengeance by an open attack upon the person of Mister McGregor. This is where the story begins (for the above details are presented in skillful and dramatic cut-backs) with the slave Rhears, knife in hand, at the door of the big house demanding to speak not to 'Marster' McGregor but to 'Mister' McGregor, a mode of address that is a rejection of McGregor's claim to mastery. In short, the story begins with an open physical challenge of slave to master.

All this and what came after was observed by the narrator, McGregor's son, as a boy of eight. But it is the man, many years later, who is telling the story and whose garrulous comments, first, clarify for us the immediate significance of that remembered action and, second, indirectly apply that significance to the narrator's own predicament. The two functions are dramatically inextricable, but for critical purposes the overt action must be the prior one.

Mister McGregor, upon hearing Rhears's challenge at the door, immediately and as a matter of course reaches for his gun, the instrument and symbol of his established authority. But what is to follow, by the interference of his wife, is an open challenge to his right to wield this authority. Her restraining hands on the gun—an action in which one of her nails draws blood from his knuckle—clearly puts the question in terms of McGregor's manhood only. Now, so challenged, he has no recourse but to risk his life in hand-to-hand combat with Rhears. And, as the narrator foresaw, "This fight was to be accorden to no rules . . . it would start fist and skull and work into a stomp and gouge." And his dramatic account fulfills our expectations of the savage struggle to come.

Obviously (although the obviousness has escaped some race-conscious readers) the story has nothing to do with slavery as such or with racial questions or dilemmas. At this point in the action, when McGregor's wife confronts him with her challenge, the area of the real conflict is made abundantly plain. Already a hint in preparation has been given. In the narrator's words, speaking of Rhears and his wife Della, "They both of'm was give to ma by her pa at the marryen; and in a way that folks don't understand no more, they somehow become a part of her." So the narrator tells us, and the full meaning of his words is borne out in terms of the ensuing action. As McGregor prepares to take Della out for her punishment, Mrs. McGregor opposes him with all the force presently at her command. " 'Mister McGregor,' come Ma's even tones, 'you're not going to punish that girl. She's mine.' " McGregor's reply, "And so are you mine, my dear," especially as elaborated in the subsequent passage dramatizing their icy mutual defiance, makes unmistakable his absolute claim to what she, just as absolutely, denies: his ultimate right to rule her in all things. Hence her challenge to him, which follows straight-away, comes like a stroke of the inevitable. Clearly enough, though it was accident that had furnished the occasion, she is using Rhears as the agent of her defiance; he is the embodiment of her will. As the narrator comments (in a comment that would be superfluous if it were not for his personal role in the story) Rhears was here by proxy to call his 'marster', and hers, to account.

The fight, rendered in all its dramatic and barbarous detail, results in the victory of Mister McGregor. There is of course no ethical question as to the means by which McGregor gains his victory, for, as stated, it was understood that the fight was to be according to no rules: Rhears's death is achieved by a stratagem in no way more savage or reprehensible than ones attempted unsuccessfully by Rhears himself. And Rhears's dying words of submission are simply: "Marster, if you hadn't got me, I'd a got you." He has lost in mortal combat; there is no question of standards kept or broken.

But Rhears's final words convey much more than this. The story's strategy has so arranged that they are not only the words of Rhears's submission but of Mrs. McGregor's also. They speak for her, and in dramatic confirmation of the fact she willingly returns the gun to her husband; Mister McGregor is established as 'marster' again in the full authority of his manhood. Now, as rendered in the final exchange on the question of Della's future, peace and concord exist once more between the wife and husband.

But what about the cost of this concord? It is in terms of this question that the story takes on what has a right to be called its tragic dimension. And this dimension is focused mainly through the role of the narrator, the son of Mister and Mrs. McGregor, who witnessed the event many years ago.

It was, as details of the story instruct us, a great many years ago— time enough for the Civil War to have come and gone, for changes that have darkened understanding of old ways of thinking, and for the narrator to consider that his life, such as it has been, is now behind him. He knows that he has failed: he uses the past tense when he reflects on his reasons for accomplishing nothing and the ruin of his health by drink. And finally there is the indication of the language he habitually uses, the colloquial and ungrammatical speech of the plain people which, by contrast with that of his parents, accents our impression of the time interval that must lie between his inherited estate and his present one.

But the narrator's manner of speech shows us more than this. It is,

in fact, the device by which his real condition is most vividly dramatized. For rather early in the story this language raises in the reader's
mind a question about the narrator, the question of how it could come
about that the rigorously formal speech to which he was reared has
left no trace of itself on his tongue. It is a question raised as soon in
the story as the reader becomes acquainted with the narrator's parents,
the putative subject of his narration, and it comes with a certain shock
of surprise. One's manner of speech is the quickest and most obvious
index to his character and, since like gets like, the reader is unprepared
to find in the narrator's parents the cultivated intelligence, dignity
and moral rigor which they so quickly reveal. Their quality is manifested in all their actions, but it is in their speech that the contrast with
their son is most clearly evident. "I have whipped Della," says Mister
McGregor to his wife, "and sent her to the field for six months. If
at the end of that time she has learned not to forget her manners, she
may take up again her duties here. In the meantime, so you will not
want, I have sent for P'niny. If you find her too old or in any way un-
suitable, you may take your choice of the young girls." And the
narrator, McGregor's son, "Rhears warn't no common field hand. He
was proud, black like the satin in widow-women's shirtwaists, and
spoiled. And his feelens was bad hurt. The day before, Pa had
whupped Della, and Rhears had had all night to fret and sull over it
and think about what was be-en said in the quarters and how glad the
field hands was she'd been whupped . . . ."

This contrast in manners of speech, then, is the strategy by which
the reader is drawn, with perfect finesse, into the real center of the
story. The ground is thus prepared for those self-revelatory remarks
of the narrator which complete the description of his present condition and also point back to the cause of it. He is, as he tells us in effect,
a loafer and a drunkard with nothing to show for his life but ruined
kidneys. He has never married because "I'm peaceful by nature," and,
he declares, the only thing capable of making him angry enough to
fight is having some one put salt in his whiskey. The inference from
this last detail, added to the fact that he is, no doubt typically, spong-
ing whiskey from his audience, suggests the way in which he is seen by
others. All his days, it is clear, are spent very much as he is spending

this one: in taverns talking the hours away, bumming drinks from auditors who sometimes get their own back with practical jokes at his expense.

It is of course the incident which the narrator relates, and what he has seen in it, that explains his life. The tale is obsessive for him: he has told it again and again, lingering over details whose significance for himself continues to resist his imperfect, because fearful, scrutiny. "It's bothered me a heap in my time, more'n it's had any right to," he says about the meaning of those looks exchanged between his parents at the critical moment when his father, accepting Mrs. McGregor's mortal challenge, relinquishes the gun. He has understood that his mother precisely meant for her husband to run so deadly a risk. He has understood also that the question was one of authority and, further, that the nature of womankind, "stuffed with dynamite" and determined to "put the man down amongst the chillun," requires for the sake of concord to be subjected. But his fear stands between his understanding of these facts and their meaning for himself. It is fear enough to parch his throat at times. Significantly those moments when the dryness comes upon him, calling for another drink, occur at the points in his narrative when he most nearly confronts the implacable character of the warfare at the very heart of life that is fully lived.

The narrator has never really confronted in this fact the meaning for himself. The reason is clear: the vision came upon him too early, in childhood, and in too sudden and terrible a form. With innocent eyes he observed the abandonment and savagery of the struggle, the brutal extinction finally, in terms of his mother's proxy, of what he conceived even then to be a part of his mother's self. And all in behalf of order between a man and woman who "had the name of be-en a mighty loven couple." Speaking of that moment when, issuing her challenge, his mother's fingernail drew blood from her husband's knuckle, the narrator says, "That blood put a spell on me." It was a spell that never would pass off, a spell whose effect was to arrest him in a condition of permanent childhood. For this is what he is, a sort of child, one who has willfully rejected, because of its terrible obligations, the assumption of full manhood. And this is why the narrative, no matter how many the thoughtful repetitions, will never quite release its final mean-

ing to the narrator. He cannot allow it. The narrative by implication
defines what he actually is, and this understanding must destroy his
last illusion of self-respect.

I have said that "Mister McGregor" has a tragic dimension. I do not
think that this would be true if the reader looked upon the narrator's
fear of life and consequent rejection as based on a perception that had
no importantly moral implication. Such a view would explain this
rejection as common cowardice merely, fear inspired by childhood
trauma. Clearly there is more to the narrator's perception. Partly the
point is made in terms of the sheer animal brutality of the struggle
("accorden to no rules"), a struggle won through a device which
by any civilized or ethical standard was not "fair." (It is a fault of the
story that Mister McGregor, with perhaps incredible courage and
certainly with damage to the point, honorably allows Rhears to re-
assume a deadly hold which he, McGregor, had broken by an accidental blow to the groin.)

However, the point is really established in the final scene of the
story between McGregor and his wife. Evidence of the carnage, the
body of Rhears, lies at their feet. Almost as an afterthought, as she
dutifully dresses her husband's wounds, Mrs. McGregor says to a
servant standing by, "And take this body out of here," in a tone that
she uses when the maid has failed to dust the room properly. Now
Della too must go, she suggests; and Mister McGregor's concurrence
brings the story to its end on a final note of harmony. Authority and,
so, concord have been restored.

But what of the cost, in moral as well as other terms? A part of the
woman, a part which the narrator respected, has been violently re-
moved, and the subsequent accord between the McGregors, callous
in its indifference to the carnage which produced it, implies acceptance
of a condition that innocence must reject. The preservation of innocence, then, rejecting guilt, rejects the requirements of manhood and
so of life itself. And this, if we are to give due weight to all implications of the narrator's tale, is an element in his withdrawal, a cause
of what he is. It is also the element which points beyond the narrator's
personal case to the tragic dimension—a moral dilemma implicit in the
nature of man himself. The student of Mr. Lytle's fiction will recog-

nize here, in this first story, a thematic implication that was to become an increasing concern of the books that were to follow.

The ultimate theme of "Mister McGregor" is well stated in W. B. Yeats's lines:

For nothing can be sole or whole
That has not been rent.

As with all of Mr. Lytle's fiction, theme is the creation of art working upon matter, and it is illuminating to see, in this impressive and intricately wrought first story, the artistic birth of the idea that was to become the seed of *The Velvet Horn.*

A Name for Evil:
A Search for Order

CHARLES C. CLARK

A Name for Evil, first published in 1947,[1] is Andrew Lytle's depiction of the effects of a perverted view of tradition. Lytle's intention in this novel has been generally misinterpreted because reviewers and critics have been primarily concerned with the discovering and pointing out of Jamesian correspondences and similarities.[2] Of course, Lytle wrote *A Name for Evil* with *The Turn of the Screw* in mind as a sort of frame; but the psychological novel he created is quite different from James's enigmatic tale. Lytle's narrator, talking of himself and his problems, leads us to an awareness of the nature of his psychosis. He shows us—never fully realizing the import of his words—how he destroys his wife and unborn child and thereby renders his life virtually meaningless in the traditional Southern-Agrarian context he has chosen for it.

Henry Brent's struggle and ultimate defeat occur within a definite time and place. Lytle, in an essay on his novel *The Velvet Horn* entitled "The Working Novelist and the Mythmaking Process," states that "there is little or no natural landscape, no recognizable cities, in myth or fairy tale. This is a crucial distinguishing feature between myth and fiction which deals with myth. They have the archetypes in common, but in fiction the action must be put in a recognizable place and society."[3] The action of *A Name for Evil* takes place in a

[1] Andrew Lytle, *A Name for Evil* (New York, 1947). The novel appears in the collection *A Novel, a Novella and Four Stories* (New York, 1958). All citations here are from the collection.
[2] See Jack De Bellis's "Andrew Lytle's *A Name for Evil*: A Transformation of *The Turn of the Screw*," *Crit.* 8 (Spring-Summer 1966), 26–40.
[3] Andrew Lytle, *The Hero with the Private Parts* (Baton Rouge, 1966), pp. 188–189.

tobacco- and grain-growing area in the southeastern part of the United States during World War II. Lytle makes good use of physical description of *The Grove*, the house and run-down farm which Henry Brent, with Ellen, his wife, buys to live on and to regenerate. *The Grove* is situated in limestone country: one of its fields has sinkholes and subterranean streams, an important fact in a key scene—but more of this later.

Brent, a no-longer-young, none-too-successful writer, tells his own story, apparently in an effort to justify himself in his own mind. The first person narration, rendered in a sometimes faltering involuted style, is suited to Brent's character.[4] He reviews and probes his thoughts and actions without realizing that the cause of his trouble is his solipsism. For it is a self-centered Henry Brent who comes to *The Grove*, which was once owned by his Civil War ancestor, one Major Brent.[5] Putting the house and farm in order, Brent believes, will delay his achievement of order in his own life: "If it was to be finished, we would have to do of necessity what once had seemed a labor of love; that is, do a great part of the work ourselves. This would take years out of our life and make of these years confusion and disorder, for a house must be so arranged that there is a place for everything" (p. 189).

The theme of Lytle's novel is suggested by the name *The Grove*. In antiquity heathen peoples planted groves which they used as places for the reception of images. Manasseh, King of Judah, blasphemed by planting a grove in honor of Baal[6] and was put to death for his sins by a jealous and wrathful Jehovah. Like Manasseh, Henry Brent worships a false god; but Brent's false god is something he has created in his mind. Brent is a creator of his world as he perceives it.[7] And in

---

[4] Thomas H. Carter says in his essay "Andrew Lytle," *South: Modern Southern Literature in its Cultural Setting*, ed. Louis D. Rubin, Jr., and Robert D. Jacobs (New York, 1961), p. 285: "Aside from the obvious ability all [Lytle's novels] reflect, they bear no superficial resemblance to one another. Since Lytle varies his texture to suit his story, they do not even have a common style."

[5] *Brent*, the past participle of the Middle English verb *brenne*, to burn, provides an appropriate surname for the Promethean-Satanic Civil War officer and for his suffering twentieth-century collateral descendant.

[6] See 2 Kings xxxi, 3: "For he built up again the high places which Hezekiah his father had destroyed; and he reared up altars for Baal...." 7: "And he set a graven image of the grove that he had made in the house...."

[7] Allen Tate, "Narcissus as Narcissus," *Collected Essays* (Denver, 1959), pp. 250–251.

this world—which for dramatic purposes Lytle, with bad country roads, makes isolated—Henry Brent, as regenerator (creator), must oppose the Satanic Major Brent, dead seventy-five years. Major Brent appears to Henry Brent and to the superstitious Negro hired man, Johnny (who imparts the history of Major Brent to the narrator as he received it from his father, one of the Major's Negroes). And so Lytle's novel, at first glance, seems to be based upon a synthesis of *Paradise Lost* and *The Turn of the Screw*.

There is, however, an important paradox in Lytle's recasting of the Edenic myth through the consciousness of Henry Brent: Brent obviously does not realize that he is interlacing his narrative with Gnostic symbols. He considers himself a traditionalist and hates the force of evil that exists in his world. This force, which threatens to destroy what he seeks to rebuild, is Major Brent. He knows that Major Brent despises tradition: Johnny has told him how the Major disinherited his sons, kept his daughter a spinster, brought the grain fields of *The Grove* to a state of perfection, and then—perversely and egoistically approving sterility—allowed the grain to stand in the fields until it rotted. Yet Henry Brent, a man plagued with a "chronic sterility" which has caused his marriage to be childless, a man as self-centered in the mid-twentieth century as Major Brent was in the mid-nineteenth, is unable to see that he is as much an enemy of the principles of the traditional society that he professes to support as was his Civil War ancestor. And, at the end of the novel, Henry Brent becomes the Major Brent he has created in his mind.

Lytle achieves this *Doppelgänger* effect by an artfully arranged sequence of scenes in which Henry Brent, narrating, philosophizing, probing himself, makes it clear that he is psychotic. Lytle gives his novel unity of place (all of the scenes take place at *The Grove*, either in the house or outbuildings or in the surrounding fields); taking the year as his unit, he gives it unity of time; and he makes all of the action, physical and psychological, lead to the catastrophe. Frequently employing dramatic irony, Lytle shows the deepening of Brent's psychosis: throughout his narrative, Brent continually condemns himself unknowingly; and, finally, holding his dead wife in his arms, he fails to realize that he has killed her.

At the beginning of his narrative, Brent tells of buying *The Grove*, of his plans to regenerate it, and of his arrival in early spring with Ellen, who refuses to allow him to carry her over the threshold because he has carried her over two thresholds already. She runs from him and slips into the house. He cannot open the door to follow her—this foreshadows her death at the end of the novel, when, startled, she flees from him.

When the narrator reprimands Johnny for not cleaning up the little room upstairs, Johnny answers that it is Major Brent's room: "He a hard man. He don't like folks projecting wid his things" (p. 178). And when the narrator asks him if he believes in ghosts, Johnny evades the question by describing in detail, with dialogue, how Major Brent relentlessly drove his sons and field hands. Major Brent is very real to the superstitious Johnny, who confuses in his mind the past (the stories his father told him) and the present. But, later in the novel, Johnny cannot see Henry Brent's nephew, Moss, though Moss is very real to Henry. Obviously, Johnny has heard no stories about the young World War II soldier, and he cannot see the shade of a man whom he has never known by reputation.

After the room-cleaning confrontation, the narrator admits that Johnny "in his way ... had shown respect for its [*The Grove's*] tradition. ... For almost the years of his life Johnny had seen owners and tenants abuse house and land. It was to his honor that he kept faith with the memory of Major Brent, the only man within his knowledge who had brought *The Grove* to its highest moment and then sustained it. In his tradition-respecting mind Johnny could find little help from the dead. Countryman that he was, he was too familiar with the natural order: the dead are dead. So dramatically ... he went beyond the laws of nature and endowed the Major with the mystery of immortality and its limitless prerogatives" (pp. 181–182). And then the narrator, with the flash of insight sometimes granted to the mentally disturbed, in his discordant style characterizes himself:

> I am not a romantic. The true romantic has hidden pockets into which his imagination secretes a drug to protect him from the common evils of the hour. I am, I was, that most unhappy of hybrids, the false romantic. With will and deliberation, and this is the essence of the difference, the false romantic ignores the true nature of reality. For the time being. And with care and half-

averted eye he hangs the veil of illusion between himself and the world. Almost from habit he believes the veil was hung by God, or in the most violent falsification of his nature, he becomes God. I say almost, for he never quite forgets what he is doing. There is this to be said for him. More often the injury done is to himself alone. The true romantic poisons the air all men breathe. (p. 182)

Lytle, then, makes it clear that he is following the Gnostic *lapis*-Christ parallel as set forth by Jung[8] to show the basis of Henry Brent's mental trouble; speaking of his reading on mythology and archetypal patterns, he tells us: "Of course reading has helped me tremendously, but I read not as a scholar but as an artist. The wonder of it is its accidental nature. . . . I happened to be reading certain authors at the time of writing [*The Velvet Horn*]—some even before I began, Frazer years ago, more recently Zimmer, Jung, particularly *Psychology and Alchemy*, and Neumann's *Origin and History of Consciousness*." [9]

After a walk with Ellen one evening, the narrator, from a distance, sees the figure of a man on the upper gallery of the house. The stranger wears a hat "wide-brimmed and black"; he has "lustrous eyes, restless, searching, boring the woods like gimlets" (p. 194). Several weeks later, Brent returns to his study one evening for his hat (Jungian symbol used by Conrad in his *Doppelgänger* story "The Secret Sharer"), sees against the windowpane the face of the uninvited visitor he has seen on the gallery, and—like James's governess-narrator— realizes that the intruder has come for someone else. As the governess frightens Mrs. Grose, Henry Brent, by putting his face against the pane at the place where the intruder's appeared to him, frightens Johnny as he enters. And then, after Brent describes the intruder to Johnny (a continuation of the governess-Mrs. Grose parallel), he asks: "Then you've seen him?" and Johnny replies: ". . . Sho', I've seed him. . . . Why that's Major Brent . . . I sees him all the time" (p. 206). Whereupon the narrator discloses his reaction to Johnny's answer:

I knew that sooner or later I would have to have it out with Johnny. . . I must discover just where Johnny's loyalty lay. I must know what he saw . . . exactly what communication existed

---

[8] C. G. Jung, *Psychology and Alchemy* (New York, 1968), pp. 345–431.
[9] Andrew Lytle, *The Hero with the Private Parts*, p. 187.

between him and the former master of *The Grove*. I come right
out with it. I do not speak of ghosts or apparitions. I speak of
Major Brent. To give *a name to evil*, if it does nothing else, limits
its range and that is the beginning of accepting it [italics supplied].
(pp. 206–207)

After talking more with Johnny about Major Brent and learning
that the Major "doan rest easy" because "all the meanness he done
plague him" (p. 208), the narrator makes this self-revealing observation: "I had been fairly certain that Johnny saw no more than all those
who believe in ghosts see, that is, the shadow of their imaginations,
filled by old stories, myths which grow like moss about the ruin
of the cornerstone." Then he adds: "But this was not what I saw.
What *I* saw, I saw alone" (p. 209).

The narrator, concerned lest the failure of his hopes to provide his
wife with material comforts and "status equal to [his] love for her"
(p. 218) threaten his manhood, works on reviews and essays in his
study "to get the material for the campaign" (p. 219). He has to mortgage the property for money to add to the money gained from the
sale of his wife's ring (the circle—the form of the mandala and Ouro-
boros of the Gnostics—becomes a dominant symbol at the end of the
novel). Thinking of the mortgage and of other time-money relationships, he says: ". . . I must have been a little mad. I dared not look
the timepiece in the face but always hurried by with averted eye . . ."
(p. 220). And in Jung's explication of the *lapis*-Christ parallel, we find
this statement:

> The Christian receives the fruits of the Mass for himself per-
> sonally and for the circumstances of his own life in the widest
> sense. The alchemist, on the other hand, receives the *fructus ar-
> boris immortalis* not merely for himself but for . . . the perfect-
> ing of the coveted substance. . . . [S]ince he is the redeemer of
> God and not the one to be redeemed, he is more concerned to
> perfect the substance than himself.[10]

Henry Brent's search for order, therefore, is dependent upon
his regeneration of *The Grove* as a mark of material success, that is,
as a measure of his manhood. "The redeemer of God and not the one
to be redeemed," he becomes a sort of creator himself, who must op-

[10] Jung, p. 352.

pose the force of evil represented in his mind by Major Brent.

For a while Henry Brent hopes to pass *The Grove* on to his brother's son, Moss, who mysteriously returns to *The Grove* from the South Pacific, where he has been serving in the war against Japan. Though Moss, in a stichomythic exchange with Henry in the study that is suggestive of a person arguing with himself, seems to doubt the existence of Major Brent, he agrees to take the night watch to protect Ellen, while Henry agrees to take the day watch. Moss is to live in an old office in the yard, his presence known to no one else except Johnny. There is subtle dramatic irony in the narrator's account of his introduction of Johnny to Moss: "I said, 'Lad, this is Johnny. He will look after your needs.' Johnny gave a quick glance to the corner where Moss was, stiffened slightly—only I would have noticed it—and then stood there with respectful dignity, hat in hand, looking not at but just to the side of Moss's position. In any other situation I would have smiled at his cunning. Nobody could trap him into admission of seeing anything." He adds: "Moss turned, smiled in his charming way, and nodded. . . . I never saw a more difficult situation handled by both parties with greater ease or discretion . . . " (p. 235). Then, in the presence of Moss, he elicits from Johnny more of the story of Major Brent's perverse attacks on tradition—how he disinherited his sons, deeded *The Grove* to his spinster daughter, and committed "that last affront to tradition, the unmarked grave" (p. 236). And musingly he sums up the situation better than he realizes: ". . . where will it lead me . . . this cold scent, but where all false trials lead—back upon myself?" (p. 238).

Shortly after this, the narrator finds Ellen in the garden, which is some distance from the house, and learns that, hoping to surprise him, she has been regenerating it. Suspecting that her interest in the garden is due to a malignant influence of Major Brent's, he arranges to have Johnny help her. At one point he almost tells her of Moss's presence at *The Grove*, but he decides not to do so. After spending idyllic afternoons at a nearby creek swimming and picnicking, and after working on the interior of the house (during which they engage in a verbal exchange about jugglers reminiscent of Shakespearean bawdy), they return to the garden to re-examine and discuss it. Johnny, on duty as Ellen's helper, supplies necrological information: projecting from the hexagonal springhouse like the spokes of a wheel are the six graves of Major Brent's wives and housekeepers, five of whom died in childbirth.

The garden is at once a Christian and a Jungian symbol: it is a symbol of Eden and man's state before the fall; and it is a mandala, an archetypal symbol of man's struggle to achieve order and of his attempt to group all the facets of life about a center—the self. According to Johnny, Major Brent mysteriously disappeared after observing his perfect, but unharvested, crop from his throne-like chair and had no grave known to man; this suggests that the sardonic Major, when he designed the garden, considered the springhouse his symbolic grave, his inversion of the fountain of life.

When Ellen leaves the garden, the narrator first fears that she is in danger from Major Brent. Later, at the house, he sees Moss, apparently hypnotized, walking toward the rotten rail of the still unrepaired balcony and realizes that it is he whom Major Brent wishes to destroy at this time. The narrator calls his nephew's name and saves him from falling to the bricks below. In another stichomythic exchange Moss exasperates the narrator by disclaiming knowledge of Major Brent; and the narrator knows that he will be hard-pressed to save Moss, his prospective heir, from the tradition-despising enemy.

As Moss and the narrator part, the latter broods about Major Brent's presence at *The Grove* and decides that the Major is being punished for the misdeeds he committed during his life: "To be neither of the world nor altogether out of it—that was his punishment" (pp. 266–267). Again he fears Major Brent has selected Ellen (woman, the "carrier" of tradition) as victim in a sacrificial act intended to win him his freedom from "the blur of mortality." The narrator enters his wife's bedroom and, jealous of Major Brent, quizzes her enigmatically, but unmercifully. To assert his manhood and his right as husband, he extinguishes the light by pressing his hand "on the hot circle [of] the lamp chimney" and takes her by force (p. 271).

The next morning, Brent, remorseful, decides that he and Ellen must flee the place; but he knows that first he must deal with Moss. He goes to the old office where Moss is staying and sees that the bed has not been slept in; he finds Johnny and commands him to take him to the place where Major Brent looked over the fields (with their perfect crop) for the last time. When they reach the field, now over-grown with trees and underbrush, Johnny refuses to enter. The narra-tor goes on alone into what is now forest (symbol of the unconscious) and sees Moss. He calls out to him, but Moss disappears into a sinkhole from which the sound of running water comes: "How long I re-mained staring I do not know, long enough to feel the dangerous pull of the subterranean sound, promising release, escape from the un-bearable, the lull of utter rest and oblivion" (p. 278). Saved from this Lethean attraction by the sudden realization that he still has some-one to protect, the narrator looks up and sees, on the other side of the sinkhole, Major Brent with the triumphant look of a carnivorous beast on his face, but "no satiety on those lips [,which] still hungered" (p. 279).

Distraught, the narrator hurries back to the house only to find that Ellen has gone to town. He tortures himself with the thought that she has gone to Major Brent. When she returns from her visit to his brother, she tells him that Moss is dead, that the Army has notified Moss's parents that he has been dead three months. This, of course, is the climax of the novel: from this point the action is falling. When, a little later, the narrator tells Johnny that Moss has been dead three months, the Negro says: "A mile don't mean nothen to a dead man" (p. 290). The narrator reaffirms that he saw Moss at *The Grove* and asks Johnny if he saw him. Johnny replies that he never saw him, that he threw the food intended for Moss to the chickens, and that he made the bed one time. At the end of the scene, Johnny suggests that Moss's ghost came to tell the narrator something: "Maybe he done tole you, kin you cipher hit" (p. 291).

After a supper in which Henry and Ellen drink a toast to the mem-ory of Moss (a sort of communion), Henry announces that "his [Moss's] death is our salvation" (p. 298) and that he is going to take Ellen away from *The Grove*, as the place is haunted. Then she tells him that she is pregnant. He is shocked that his "chronic sterility" should have disappeared so suddenly. Regarding the pregnancy as a sort of miracle, he comments: "Now I knew that my good daemon had deliberately led me to *The Grove*. Not to escape the accident of the world but to come into my own. I was now to be the head of a family, a true family, returned to my proper place, and that place physically and spiritually of a sound and explicable history" (p. 300). As everything in Henry Brent's life revolves about himself, he thinks in the first-person singular on such an occasion.

Brent relates that he remained in a state of elation during the remainder of the fall season (his changes in mood suggest manic-depressive tendencies). With insight that seems uncanny to the neighbors and to Johnny, he harvests the tobacco crop just before a frost which damages the crops of others. And, one night in the barn, where the tobacco is being cured, he sees Major Brent again: "His face, as red as the coals he was hovering over, distinctly carried an appeal, but it was so loathsome in its naked directness he must have seen how it repelled me. In a flash he was threatening me, and the cold fury of it left me shivering in the heat of the barn" (p. 305).[11]

Now certain that Major Brent threatens the unborn child, the narrator, again referring to himself as a false romantic, asks: "How was I to know that I had put myself in the way of the past and the future, bemused by the mad fancy that I could reach into history and regenerate, a function proper only to a god? . . . it came to me with the suddenness of revelation: was not my idea the obverse of Major Brent's act, with the difference that he had died unrepentant and the vanity of his act bound him in torment to the shadowy air of the place, haunting it until that time he could work his release? . . . Unpurged, unregenerate spirit that he was, he would know only to seek his release through a repetition of the original error" (p. 308). But gleefully reflecting that phantoms are beyond history and only think they may perpetuate it, the narrator goes to the house to warn Ellen, who is, of course, quite upset when he finally tells her that he has seen Major Brent.

Early in December, the narrator's brother, a successful businessman, arrives from town in response to a letter from Ellen. He reprimands the narrator for telling ghost stories to his pregnant wife and promises to supply the couple a house in town.

But in January, shortly after Christmas ("We spent a quiet Christmas. . . ." [p. 319]: the only statement the narrator makes concerning

---

[11] Here Lytle is using the Dantean-Shakespearean-Miltonic representation of punishment by heat and cold. In many parts of *A Name for Evil* he interweaves descriptions of the four elements (important in mandala symbolism, as well as in Renaissance poetry).

either of the two most important days in the Christian calendar), fate in the form of weather delays the removal to town. Rain, sleet, snow, and a steadily dropping temperature cover everything with ice and snow. The narrator takes Ellen to the garden to show her its beauty, perfected by snow and ice, and made eerie by fog. They become lost. In an attempt to find the gate, he leaves her in the vicinity of the springhouse (with its Christian-Ouroboros serpent-fountain and its six graves). Unable to find the gate, he begins to move in circles to find Ellen. Suddenly he sees her, head down, apparently listening to something. He screams her name in warning. Startled, she looks at him, backs away, saying, "No, no, no." Then the narrator sees Major Brent, dressed as a bridegroom, reaching forth his arms for her. Shouting, the narrator dashes forward. Ellen leaps upon the rotten platform of the springhouse and falls through it. The narrator rushes to her side and lifts her: "Already I knew what it was I held in my arms, and I knew that at last Major Brent had triumphed and I was alone" (p. 327).

The circling that the narrator does to find his wife is, of course, symbolic of his solipsism, as is the mandala-shaped garden in which he moves. At the end of the novel he is at the center of his spiral. Probably Ellen, a frail woman, highly nervous because of her husband's mental condition, her pregnancy, and the eeriness of the garden, thinks, when she sees her husband just before she falls to her death, that she is seeing Major Brent. And, in effect, Henry Brent has become Major Brent: he is the jaguar leaping for his own image.[12]

One critic has said of *A Name for Evil* that "this novel seems the best single refutation of Agrarian-traditionalist positions that has been produced either by its [sic] enemies or its supporters. . . ."[13] This statement is wrong. In *A Name for Evil* Andrew Lytle depicted what he intended to depict—the fatal effects of a distorted, private view of tradition. To do this, he used what he had learned from Henry James (form and need to dramatize), from Jung and other psychologists (archetypal symbolism), and from Joyce (epiphany and secular communion). But, most of all, he used what he had learned, through experience, of a people and a country.

12 Allen Tate, "Ode to the Confederate Dead," 11. 82–83.
13 John M. Bradbury, *The Fugitives: A Critical Account* (Chapel Hill, 1958), p. 271.

The Quality of Richness: Observations on Andrew Lytle's *The Long Night*

H. L. WEATHERBY

EVERY WRITER HAS his characteristic gift, a particular quality or flavor which makes his works his own and nobody else's. In the case of Andrew Lytle that gift is what I would call his *richness*—diversity, fullness, plenitude. At least it is this quality, I find, which draws me back to his novels and stories, and it is the vividness of individual scenes and of the fictional world in which those scenes are set which I remember long after I have forgotten the details of plot and names of characters.

Anyone familiar with Mr. Lytle's work will recognize at once what I am talking about. Consider, for instance, a story like "Jericho, Jericho, Jericho"; with the very mention of the name dozens of sharp details crowd the memory—ground so rich it would make your feet greasy to walk on it; the almost pleasant smell of a distant polecat; the stench of wet hounds steaming by the fire; Brother Jack with his cleft palate and his taste for whiskey, himself cut in two by chain shot at Murfreesboro; macassar oil dripping from a young lover's locks and down on his collar; the rustle of old love letters in a basket quilt; the half-tester of the bed opening out like a sunrise above Mrs. Mc-Cowan's head where she lies dying; white naked bodies dragged by horses over rough ground; sweat shining on a black face in the lamplight; white cotton fields under an intense blue sky. If these are not exact, it is because I have listed them from memory, and I have done so to prove my point: that the details stick, and they stick not only in the mind but in the senses. I read "Jericho, Jericho, Jericho" for the first time sixteen years ago; these details have been with me ever since.

However, sharp details alone do not constitute all I mean by richness in fiction, for a novel can never be simply a collection of vivid fragments; the details have to mean something, have to have a place in the novel as a whole. It is true that the sights and smells at Long Gourd would not stick in the memory were they not vividly realized, each in its own right; but at the same time they would prove to be equally tenuous if they had no significance to the meaning of the story. So here we see that richness of the sort I am describing requires a perilous balance. On the one hand the details that constitute a fictional world must have life and vividness in themselves, a kind of existential autonomy. Each character, each place, each scent must be what St. Thomas Aquinas calls an "act of being" in its own right, not simply a mask or image in which the general "idea" of the story clothes and manifests itself. At the same time these individual acts of being must co-inhere to form a world which has being or unity as a whole, and neither the individual acts of being nor the being of the whole can be sacrificed.

There is a great deal of good fiction which makes a different sort of demand. In Conrad's novels, for instance, the integrity of the fictional world depends largely upon the unity of plot and theme. It is not the details of the foreground but the underlying idea which gives his work unity. Even his most vivid seascapes lack independent existence, lack being. They are there to illustrate an idea or to create a mood, and we seldom remember them except when we recapture the subjective experiences of those characters for whom they have significance. In Mr. Lytle's world, on the other hand, people, things, and places stand up and declare their unique existences, and theme and plot are generated by those declarations, not by the idea. There is really no idea as such in "Jericho, Jericho, Jericho," nothing which in an abstract statement would make much sense. There is rather a place with its people, sights and smells. Nothing happens simply in the mind, for sense images nourish the whole fabric of the story. Consequently it is impossible to abstract some purely intellectual content from the story, and any effort to do so in memory calls us back immediately to place, sight, taste and smell.

We can say, therefore, that the principle of richness, the actuality of being, in Mr. Lytle's fiction is also the principle of unity or meaning in that fiction. Take, for instance, *The Long Night*; and as a particularly good example of what I mean, the sequence of events which terminates in Damon Harrison's death. Damon is a complex character involved in a complex situation, and Mr. Lytle makes no effort to simplify either character or circumstance in order to conform them to some preconceived idea of what they ought to mean. Damon's father, Quintus Harrison, has gambled away his family plantation in the Alabama Black Belt and has been forced to begin life again, and in straitened circumstances, in the hill country of Coosa County. His wife resents the loss and the new life bitterly, primarily because she sees that Damon, now eighteen, is being drawn into the life of the hill country, "the Buyckville world," which is foreign to his blood and breeding. She is not simply a snob; and her apprehensions are ultimately justified, for it is Damon's relation with that community which costs him his life. On the other hand Damon gains something by that relationship and by dying in the way he does that his mother, in her seclusion, loses.

From the time we first meet him we follow Damon's progress from the fringes toward the center of the community. His very genes are clearly an obstacle to that progress, for his classical name, his "reckless blue eyes," his heroic, if adolescent, bearing bespeak the "blood," and distinguish him from the hill-country people to whom he has become attached. On the other hand he is in the process of winning an entrance into this new life in which he finds himself. The mule-breaking scene is an instance, for that is the occasion on which Damon wins his spurs; it is his initiation into a society which breaks mules rather than horses, though the latter is the kind of world to which he was born and in which he properly belongs.

His relationship with the community is strengthened further when he falls in love with Ruth Weaver, for she belongs to the blood and soil of Coosa County. Lest we forget that fact of her belonging we always see her in a family group, chasing a swarm of bees or helping prepare a funeral supper. This latter scene is particularly interesting, for it is here that the complexity of Damon's situation (in fact of the entire novel) is brought into view. The whole Buyckville community is present at the funeral, and, in one sense, that whole community and its action have been the cause of death. The dead are Brother Macon and Ruth's cousin, Alf Weaver, both shot while acting as members of a posse formed to capture Pleasant McIvor. Pleasant has vowed to kill all the men who were involved in his father's murder, which means he must exterminate a large segment of the Buyckville community, apparently including Damon. Now, two of his victims lie in the Weavers' front room and the rest of the community gathers for their burial. The same body which has killed unjustly and earned by doing so the severe justice of Pleasant's vengeance now gathers in genuine communal piety to bury its dead.

The paradoxical nature of the situation brings us back to the principle of richness or actuality, for this complex, self-contradictory community (and all communities are complex and self-contradictory) is defined, not by the simplicity of an idea, but by the multiplicity and contradictory profusion of its actual being. Everything which belongs to that being is present at the Weavers' house and is brought to life with Mr. Lytle's characteristic vividness: the cedar buckets of fresh-drawn water, the smell of boiling coffee, two brown hams, four freshly baked cakes, four loaves of new bread and others still baking. These details suggest richness and goodness and leave no question that the community in its plenitude is to be considered as good, as a center of life and value in the novel. Yet the occasion of the gathering is violent death, and other equally vivid details suggest the very antithesis of life and fullness. The two brown hams, "rising from their drippings," are symbols of hospitality and order, yet they have been sent by Mr. Lovell, who is the truly guilty party in Cameron McIvor's murder and who is therefore indirectly responsible for the deaths of Macon and Weaver; and Lem Botterall, the sheriff and the security of the community, who wakes piously with the dead and attends unselfishly to the unpleasant job of their laying out, is also deeply involved with the same guilt.

Damon is still on the edge of this plenitude and complexity. He is drawn to the funeral primarily on account of Ruth, and he "hangs around," waiting for a chance to see her. We are reminded of his alienation when a large woman, almost an emblem of plenitude in herself, "her stomach rolling from under the dark calico apron," asks him, "whose boy are you?" When he answers, "Mr. Quintus Harrison's," she registers, in a friendly way, the fact that the Harrisons do not belong: "Lawd, I've heard about him, but this is the fust I've seen any of his folks" (p. 153). Meanwhile Damon's initiation is proceeding. He is asked to bring water to the "laying-out room," and when he arrives, he finds that Beatty, Botterall and Simmons, who are doing the good office of washing the bodies, are already tipsy. They have pulled the clothes off Brother Macon's corpse and gotten his feet in the tub. At the moment Damon arrives with the water "he saw the grayish-brown figure leaning grotesquely against the mantelpiece. The body was thin and drawn, and it had the cold shine of death. The icy eyes stared into the room, and the beard hung softly down. From the hole in the stomach a black stream of dried blood had spread down the inside of a thigh, streaking the calf, to the twisted toes" (pp. 162–163). Damon must dump the water in the tub at the corpse's feet.

The point is quite clear: that just as the community involves both good and evil in inextricable connection with one another, it also involves life and death in the same close bond. In fact the bond is so close and the relationship so complex that it can never be expressed simply as idea; it must be shown in the very details which in their actuality, their "liveness," constitute the complexity. Whiskey, good food, hospitality, pious and impious acts, falling in love, killing and dying are all parts of the same pattern of experience. The meaning of the pattern resides in the life of the details which make it up, and at the same time the life of those details gains its meaning from the whole. Therefore, to be drawn into the pattern as Damon is being drawn is to be brought under the power of actual events and people, and it is a measure of Mr. Lytle's richness that we cannot say that drawing is simply good or simply evil. Damon's mother has defined it as simply evil, and her judgment is clearly an over-simplification. On the other hand Damon's choice proves to be less than simply good.

In the event, his initiation brings him life and death in close juxta-position. After supper he meets Ruth and they slip away to the woods together. There on the verge of his greatest happiness he is murdered by Pleasant McIvor for his part in the community which has killed Pleasant's father. In other words, Damon is killed for belonging to a world which in the person of Ruth Weaver promises him the life and happiness which his mother and father in their exile have lost. He probably expresses the sentiment of Ruth's own household and of the others gathered there for the funeral when he says that Cameron McIvor was an "old son-of-a-bitching nigger stealer" (p. 172); and immediately he feels Pleasant's dagger strike his side. To make the matter more complex still the last words he hears are the fruit of belonging to the very community, the belonging to which has killed him: "Oh, Damon, Damon . . . I'll love you all my life" (p. 173).

Damon's role in the book is as a foil to Pleasant, and having examined the former's situation we are now in a position to see how its complexity contributes to the meaning of the novel. Consider for a moment Pleasant's situation at the moment he drives the knife into Damon's side; it is potentially more complicated than that of the boy he kills. He has vowed to revenge his father's murder and to restore thereby the family honor. In other words he, too, is representative of a community, that of his own kin, and in his case too the sources of life and death are closely linked. Had he not felt bound as he did, as he had to be, by family honor, he would have been spared the deadly course on which he is set. However, Pleasant's course is different from Damon's; where the latter has been drawing closer and closer to the heart of the complex actuality which constitutes the community, Pleasant has drawn progressively further away. He is even alienated from the family whose honor he is defending, for, on the whole, they have repudiated the course he has taken. We begin to see that he is in a genuinely tragic dilemma. To sustain the honor of his family, which is the principle of community, he must sacrifice that very principle and become an alien, a "loner." That is the path he chooses, and one way of interpreting the choice would be to say that he repudiates that richness and complexity of human existence which is the measure of reality in Mr. Lytle's fictional world.

Thus, at the wake, while Damon is inside, becoming embroiled in the web of actuality which at once makes him and undoes him, Pleasant is outside looking in, secure but possibly damned in his abstraction and simplicity. Simmons saw him and, significantly, thought him a "hant"; for Pleasant has learned the "menace of secret places" (p. 105). He has withdrawn from the richness of actuality and thereby gained a deadly advantage over men like Botterall or Damon who "live by daylight," whose freedom and maneuverability are hampered by the web of real being. He has learned the simplicity of singlemindedness and loneness, "to be at ease in the dark." "To know what the long night meant. That was the secret of vengeance" (p. 106).

Fortunately for his soul's good Pleasant's life does not end in that moment of simplicity when he drives the knife into Damon's side; however, his subsequent development and his ultimate repentance need not concern us here. What does concern us is that the sense of richness, of particularity and actuality, which is the earmark of Mr. Lytle's style, is also the key to his meaning. For it should now be clear that the conflict between the community and the exile, which is Mr. Lytle's persistent theme in all his fiction, is realized, not in terms of the idea or of merely allegorical or illustrative images, but as a conflict between the richness of actual being and the denial, repudiation, of that richness. As such it becomes a conflict between existence and its negation, for to exist, really to be, is to be part of the insoluble complexity of a particular, local state of affairs. The only way to simplify real life, to separate the good from the evil, is to undo the very structure of being, and that will only be accomplished by the angels at the last day. Pleasant's is a familiar role in literature, that of the scourge in the revenger's tragedy; he attempts to take the judgment, the undoing of actuality, on himself.

It is Mr. Lytle's considerable accomplishment as a novelist that he has undertaken no such vengeance on his material; that he has allowed the real existence of things in all their immediacy, diversity and locality to bring their life into his art. The fact that he has done so accounts for the remarkable warmth of his fiction, for the way he appears to love his characters, places, sights and smells, and to brood over them, to hover them, as Mrs. McCowan hovers the animals, fields and fences of Long Gourd, to embrace them even when they are weak and evil and, in a sense, to forgive them. I do not think the word *love* in such a context is too strong; for, after all, it is the unique capacity of Charity to love all men and all things simply because they are, because each is an act of being created by and contingent upon pure existence itself, who is God. Such love demands the forgiveness of one's enemies, and that, in the final analysis, is the point of *The Long Night*.

The Whole and the Parts:
Initiation in "The Mahogany Frame"

EDWARD KRICKEL

CRITICS HAVE LARGELY ignored the work of Andrew Lytle. Since ours is an age that seems to need the intermediary assurances of the critic, Lytle's brilliance as an artist and his solid achievement are therefore little known. John L. Stewart, acclaimed by Northern reviewers as the definitive historian of the Fugitive and Agrarian episodes, easily dismissed him as minor. This may have been on the slight bulk of Lytle's work, but the critic seems to have disliked the personality of the young author that he exhumed and, in addition, was embarrassed over "The Hind Tit," which he does not understand. By his own account, he has put himself with those readers of the early thirties who were of surpassing modernity and consummate sophistication, the sort that transformed *Radix omnium malorum est Cupiditas* by substituting *Rusticitas*. O brave new world! Alexander Karanikas in a generally bad book said even less. John Bradbury, author of two volumes that touched on Lytle, said more, but he hardly improved the situation either by the degree of his perception or in his expression of what he saw.

These critical derelictions have done a harm not easy to excuse. Partially from the lack of critical percipience, Lytle's work has been the property of those who met him and came under his personal spell, his friends, and a happy few of the discriminating. The critical accounts point to "influences," and the author himself points to some they never thought of, but adds:

> To put such store by influences, then, is to make a basic mistake about the nature of an art; it is to reduce it to a rational act. This attitude also falsifies the thing made by confusing what is

42

unique to it, the artist's own way of seeing and doing, with the common grounds of experience any artist of necessity must draw upon.[1]

The happy few more nearly accord with Caroline Gordon's remarks on *The Velvet Horn*: "He breaks most of the rules and emerges with a novel which is beautiful and terrible and utterly his own. I suspect that it is a landmark in American fiction. I do not know any other novel like it." Since a handful of stories is part of his achievement, also generally not known, I propose to examine "The Mahogany Frame." It was given that title when collected in *A Novel, A Novella and Four Stories* (1958); on first publication in 1945, it was called "The Guide."

Of Lytle's own essays, Allen Tate has said that they "are not like any other literary criticism of our time," for as critic he "brings to the analysis of works by other writers the same insight that enables him to write about his own. He writes about *Madame Bovary* as if he had written Flaubert's masterpiece."[2] Ideally, a critic should do as much for Lytle, but one may not at will duplicate the feat. It seems fair enough by less arduous measure to say that Bradbury is inadequate on "The Mahogany Frame." He sees influences right off; ". . . like most of Lytle's stories," it

> has a derivative ring, this time of such Faulkner stories as "The Bear," and of the Hemingway stories of Nick Adam's [*sic*] earlier experiences. . . . Like its models, it is the story of the maturation of a young boy in intimate association with nature.[3]

To him it is a story about duck hunting on Reelfoot Lake, and the atmosphere is evoked well. However, it resembles the Faulkner story "in its thematic concern with tradition." In order to question Bradbury more fairly, I quote him:

> The young protagonist enters on his initiatory experience with the ideal image of his great-grandfather before him. His uncle and the guides on the lake seem to conspire to destroy the image

[1] "Foreword," *A Novel, A Novella and Four Stories* (New York, 1958), p. xiii. Quotations from "The Mahogany Frame" come from this book and are not footnoted.

[2] "Foreword," *The Hero with the Private Parts* by Andrew Lytle (Baton Rouge, 1966), p. xiv, p. xvii.

[3] John Bradbury, *The Fugitives: A Critical Account* (Chapel Hill, 1958), p. 269.

.... The revelation occurs when the boy suddenly sees the uncle looking at him with his great-grandfather's eyes. The recognition of continuity of a tradition, however fallible, as traditions must be, becomes therefore the burden of the story—and the reader of Warren's novels will have discovered an additional source for Lytle's fiction.[4]

What the critic thinks the initiation is, what happens to the boy in relation to his forebear, what he sees in his uncle are still mysteries after one reads Bradbury. The influence thesis seems no profounder than that Faulkner and Hemingway preceded Lytle; for that matter, Hemingway must have influenced "The Bear," since his Nick Adams stories came before the Mississippian's work. All three must have influenced the hunting passages in Durrell's Alexandria books—at least by this logic. Why stop here when a whole 19th century full of initiation fiction awaits in Goethe, Balzac, Dickens, Keller, and the rest? Nor am I sure what Bradbury regards as "tradition." Nothing good, clearly. Rather than seeing the influence of Warren, he might ponder Donald Davidson's essay "Poetry as Tradition," and perhaps he would discover there a possibility of not one more influence but a source of strength in the Southern tradition that is behind all three. Let us be charitable and believe that Bradbury's space was limited and be done with him.

Lytle regards "the loss of innocence or the initiation of youth into manhood" as an archetypal experience and acknowledges that "The Mahogany Frame" is such a story. A youth goes through a series of events and gains new knowledge. The term "initiation" is used so loosely as to mean not much more than that, even though the same thing is true of most fiction. Usually, however, we intend by it those adolescent crises with sex or growing beyond childhood's illusions by other means. Harriet R. Holman suggests a distinction between two kinds of initiation stories; in one the child is "initiated with violence into a world of men—an ugly world full of unearned suffering and hatred and loss." The other

> involves a child exposed to pain of a personal, a private kind, not public or violent or readily recognized by others. And out of this quiet experience come new values which enrich the old without

4 *Ibid.*, p. 270.

displacing or wrecking them. It implies acceptance, endurance, and most significant, continuity—continuity of person, of family, of society, of values.

The protagonist, by the strength of inward qualities, "adapts and endures without suffering disorientation." [5]

I wonder if a distinction should be made between "loss of innocence" and "initiation." The terms do overlap, but not entirely. If "disorientation" occurs and nothing else, is the story a true initiation? Having borrowed the term from the study of myth and archaic cultures, we tend to use it more metaphorically than literally. What is a formal initiation in a traditional society? In the hope that it will aid clarification, I turn to the accounts of Joseph Campbell in *The Hero with a Thousand Faces* and *The Masks of God: Primitive Mythology.* His example is that of an Aranda aborigine in Central Australia; yet drawing from many sources, he insists that "analogies—even minute analogies—exist far too numerously between the mythological traditions of the higher and lower cultures to be dismissed as the mere fall of chance...." [6] I think his account can also serve as a measure for initiation in fiction.

All initiations are fabulous voyages. The rites are celebrations of wholeness whereby a youth is transformed into a new being at once human and divine. He is made to know a fullness that partakes of all living men, of ancestors, of gods, of animals and plants, a being that transcends time, yet dwells in it moment by moment. Ritually, he is present and participant at the first creation. The particular forms are those fashioned out of history and local circumstances, but the content is universal human nature. As Campbell says, "Ritual is mythology made alive, and its effect is to convert men into angels." The end is that "archaic man was not a man at all, in the modern, individualistic sense of the term, but the incarnation of a socially determined archetype." This "apotheosis" was effected in the rites of initiation. [7] By means of the ceremony, participants become walking "epiphanies of a cosmic mystery." [8]

[5] "A Measure for the Story of Initiation," *SAMLA Bulletin*, 33 (November 1968), 24–26.
[6] *The Masks of God: Primitive Mythology* (New York, 1959), p. 112.
[7] *Ibid.*, p. 118.   [8] *Ibid.*, p. 179.

In general, as Campbell puts it:

> The tribal ceremonies of birth, initiation, marriage, burial, in-
> stallation, and so forth, serve to translate the individual's life-
> crises and life-deeds into classic, impersonal forms. They disclose
> him to himself, not as this personality or that, but as the warrior,
> the bride, the widow, the priest, the chieftain; at the same time
> rehearsing for the rest of the community the old lesson of the
> archetypal stages. All participate in the ceremonial according to
> rank and function. The whole society becomes visible to itself as
> an imperishable living unit. Generations of individuals pass, like
> anonymous cells from a living body; but the sustaining, timeless
> form remains. By an enlargement of vision to embrace this super-
> individual, each discovers himself enhanced, enriched, supported,
> and magnified. . . . [T]he man or woman who can honestly say
> that he or she has lived the role—whether that of priest, harlot,
> queen, or slave—*is* something in the full sense of the verb *to be.*[9]

Further, initiation and installation rites "teach the lesson of the essential oneness of the individual and the group; seasonal festivals open a
larger horizon." [10]

In particular, however, the initiation of a young male has a masculine
exclusiveness. The youth is brought into his adult masculinity. Though
a woman bore "his temporal body," now the men will "bring him to
spiritual birth," as Campbell puts it. The secret revelation of these
rites is outside the ken of child or woman. Yet part of the ordeal is
specifically erotic and intends to direct "the boy's pliant mind and
will . . . forward to the image of his manhood with an earthly wife." [11]
Attending these "rituals of transformation" is a change of appearance;
the physical body is "transformed by the ordeals into an ever-present
sign of a new spiritual state." In societies "where the body is no longer
naked and mutilated, new clothes and ornaments are assumed . . . to
symbolize and support the new spiritual state. . . ." [12]

There are three stages, Campbell abstracts, in all initiation rites.
These are "separation from the community, transformation (usually
physical as well as psychological), and return to the community in
the new role." [13] He cautions us on one important point—myth is

---

[9] *The Hero with a Thousand Faces* (New York, 1949), pp. 383–384.
[10] *Ibid.*, p. 384.   [11] *Masks*, pp. 89–90.
[12] *Ibid.*, p. 117.   [13] *Ibid.*, p. 116.

local in its forms. Initiation is induction into a particular local group
and its cosmology, "not to any merely open, uncommitted manhood,
but specifically to a certain style of thought and feeling, impulse and
action...." Every local system has "a long history behind it of a
particular sort of social experience and cannot be explained in general
psychological terms" because of its close adjustment to "specific,
geographically determined conditions of existence." Its ideas have
been derived from long ages of "meditations on a recognized natural
order of the living world." Therefore, "no functioning mythological
system can be explained in terms of the universal images of which it
is constituted," because the history of a particular culture is involved.[14]

The components of a traditional initiation, then, are: ceremonial
transformation of the individual, in terms of both ultimates and local
conditions and history, giving him new being and, it follows, new
knowledge which includes new dimensions of time as well as new
concepts of himself, life, and society, a change symbolized by a new
physical appearance or costume. In "The Mahogany Frame" most of
these elements appear in some form. The local particulars and Lytle's
artistic use of them are to be explained. Before that, we must look at
his comments on the story for the clarification they might give.

The author tells us that "the boy's initiation happens 'by accident,'
through the ritual of hunting, itself debased...." In our culture "we
do not formally instruct our young men. What there is of it is private
and accidental." Though it is an archetypal experience when youth
is inducted into manhood, "the young men of different societies will
respond in various ways." In the case of this story, our "lack of
ritual limited, at the very start, the archetypal conflict...." Finally,
the change in the boy which "comes at the end in a shock of illumination is the measure of how he achieves maturity without formal
guidance." [15]

Once again, Campbell's remarks are pertinent:

> ... it would certainly seem that when an essentially cerebral em-
> phasis preponderates in the schooling of the young, as it does in
> our highly literate society, an alarming incidence of serious failure
> is to be expected in the difficult passage of the critical threshold

---

[14] *Ibid.*, p. 90.   [15] Lytle, "Foreword," p. xiii.

from the system of sentiments proper to infancy to that of the responsibilities of the hour. . . .[16]

From Lytle's comments just quoted, I single out "the lack of ritual" and "the ritual of hunting, itself debased." I take him to mean that hunting is not specifically related to our society by being consciously designed and used to effect the transformation of the young. Hunting as part of a rite of formal initiation may be as self-conscious and profound as the pattern Campbell finds:

> One is linked to one's adult role . . . by being identified with a myth—participating actually, physically, oneself, in a manifestation of mythological forms, these being visibly supplied by the roles and patterns of the rite, and the rite, in extension, supporting the form of society.[17]

I take it, further, that in any modern society hunting is only remotely related to its primordial beginnings; therefore, what it can carry as a literary device is limited. The most likely thing is something about the activity itself—one is initiated into the mystique of the hunt, which long ago lost its aspect of necessity and as a result its religious signification. Still, the aura is there of the distant time when hunting was ritual and necessity, the hunted both god and substance of the god freely given as food for his ritually anointed.

The hunt in "The Mahogany Frame" is the first duck hunt of the nameless boy whose point of view gives us the story. His mentor for the occasion is his maternal uncle, who had decided the boy was old enough to go and asked him. The boy sees men who came "out of some urgent need they did not rightly understand—all of them now and in his great-grandfather's day, were guided, were governed by the instincts of a bird." Here is the predictable-unpredictable aspect of nature, the basic analogical paradigm that remains true for the life of even modern civilized man. These men do not know their own natures; their society has repressed parts instead of using them creatively. "Nevertheless," as Campbell points out, "the dominant motive in all truly religious . . . ceremonial is that of submission to the inevitables of destiny—and in the seasonal festivals this motive is particularly apparent." [18] These men lack a religion.

---

[16] *Masks*, p. 92.   [17] *Ibid.*, p. 117.   [18] Campbell, *Hero*, p. 384.

The situation the boy finds is different only in degree from his great-grandfather Laus's day. Then too hunting was more pleasure than necessity, though the aura of "time-transcending ritual" was also present. The chief difference for the boy is the blatantly commercialized thing the hunt has become. He believes this was not the case when Laus hunted here, but that (its truth aside) is part of his idealization of the past. For if the action proper is the boy's experiences on the hunt, the enveloping action is the highly commercialized world of the duck hunt and by easy extension the entire commercialized modern world. The guides work for money: "All of this, Uncle Bomar?" . . . . "Yeah, I know. It's too damm much, but it's what they charge." The boy's guide, Goosetree, tells him, "There's no money in guiding," and does not want his son to do it. Goosetree has bought a bargain place nearby which he plans to rent to sojourning couples. "There'll be money in it." He brags about his bargain.

The contrast between the two guides is pertinent. It is made in several ways. Tommy is a kind of lost bard. While drunk he tells a story of his background in which he claims to be the son of a Jewish trader and an Indian woman, and when he was eleven to have killed the drunken father. This story is not true literally, I presume. The alleged father was a man of commerce and not faith. His impulses were destructive of himself and his offspring. I see in the conflict debased religious and intellectual values played off against the instinctive and natural, these forces represented by the respective characters of the father and mother. Tommy himself is instinctive and natural, full of emotion and wildness in marked contrast to the other guide. Jokes are made about his abiding interest in fornication; he drinks to excess. When he and Bomar fail to get ducks, it is as though he blames "the incomprehensible workings of Fate." He is a man potentially pious but corrupted, a traditionalist without a tradition. His story, evidently representing his dilemma in the world, is a kind of wish fulfillment; and, though a tall tale, it is symbolically true. The same conflict is dramatized throughout the enveloping action.

The other guide, Goosetree, is essentially a petty bourgeois, a man for all seasons of the commercial calendar. His single answer is money. He is the man of calculation, where Tommy is the man of feeling; he does not drink. His methods of hunting are calculated and methodical and more successful than Tommy's. Having clocked the movements of the ducks, he checks his watch with pride when they appear on schedule. Where Tommy is a satyr misbegotten into a crass time, Goosetree is flourishing. He is Shaw's Nicola in *Arms and the Man,* the realist; he is Lopahin in Chekhov's *The Cherry Orchard,* the practical man of the future; he is Huguenau in Broch's *The Sleepwalkers,* the man without principle. The contrast between the two guides is emphasized by their eyes, which are traditionally the most spiritual of the senses, the light of the soul. Tommy's are out of harmony with the rest of his appearance; the best part of him, they make him look like a pirate. He is "at least human and it was somehow because of his eyes." Watching the sky, his eyes "absorbed it like a blotter." Goosetree, on the other hand, looks at the sky covetously, as though to use it. Tommy's eyes look at the sky with awe, Goosetree's skin it. The boy refers to them as "Tommy" and "Mr. Goosetree."

The commercial point is further emphasized by the distance the boy must go in order to participate in even this "debased ritual," comparable to the distance the hunters have to travel in Faulkner's "Delta Autumn," after the timber interests have cut down the forest. En route the boy and his uncle stop at a hotel in Center for a few hours of sleep. The proprietor uses himself as a kind of decoy; he is dressed as a hunter and talks glibly of the shooting in hopes of luring real hunters to buy his accommodations. Tommy twits them coarsely about their stop and adds, "And they'll steal there, too." Again, he is symbolically right. The distance to the wilderness is suggestive of things like the gulf between modern civilization and fundamentals. The enveloping action brings this out repeatedly. Mythically, this journey is the boy's withdrawal from society so that he might undergo his initiation.

In such a context the boy's initiation would, of necessity, only be an accident. Just the smaller aspects of the hunt are consciously held by the participants. Nobody knew or intended what happened to the boy. His access of insight might well not have happened. Bomar at least sensed the youth's readiness at the threshold, since he asked him to go this time after having refused his childish wheedles in the past: "The invitation was plainly Bomar's way of accepting him as a man. Bomar did not take boys duck shooting." And the boy himself "felt that at last he was ready for a man's pleasures and responsibilities." But he does not know what these are, nor how he should behave, and nobody tells him. There is no formal induction into a given body of lore and set of objects that comprise the symbols of a cosmology.

The detail of the maternal uncle is suggestive. In matriarchies he carries out male roles in the rituals. The modern South, obviously the setting for "The Mahogany Frame," is still enough of a matriarchy for the point to be worth considering. In a true matriarchy, woman as queen or goddess enacts ceremonially the universal principles acknowledged by all; in a debased matriarchy, woman acts out masculine roles that are not true to her nature and performs them with uncertainty and misunderstanding. Here more than in eternal feminine nature we get caprice, cruelty, and the rest. Women have dominated the boy's childhood. He must now learn to view the situation from an adult male point of view.

From the life of Laus, the boy's mother derived saws that are supposedly moral wisdom to fit him for a civilized life. He becomes aware that these are dry, abstract, and partial, lacking in the juices of actual life: "And so it came to him that from his mother he got most of the admonitions but the stories he had from his grandfather or from Jake." The men, on the other hand, take up the stories of Laus that bring out the wildness, the escape from the civilized restraints. Their vision corresponds to a part of their own natures constricted by civilization but not eliminated. This they share with the guide Tommy and other hunters. Obviously, their sexual natures are involved. One hunter has evidently carried on an affair at the Lake with Nelly the waitress. The wilderness and the hunt, then, have sexual qualities. And what would a male initiation be without sexuality?

Bomar, about whom there are whispered scandals in the family, is bitter toward women. In context his remarks seem to mean that he is unable to reconcile sexual abandon with the civilized requirements for sexuality. In larger terms, the problem is that of the adult pleasures and responsibilities the boy felt himself ready for. By skillful timing, Laus was able to have both, Bomar claims enviously. In due time Laus was converted to Christianity, presumably his way to reconcile these dualities, though that point seems lost on Bomar, for he regards the conversion with cynicism. The Christian way appears not possible for Bomar. To the pagan Tommy he makes fun of Laus's conversion, but his words reveal his knowledge of the forms of the kind of initiation that Christian conversion is. Will it come to him in time, too? Perhaps, but not any time soon.

There are ways of demonstrating one's masculinity other than fornication, but in this modern non-ritualistic hunt some men blatantly acknowledge both its sexual aspect and its degenerated form by bringing women with them—women not their wives. This is another sign of the modern confusion; women on the hunt mean that the lines of conduct have become muddled, not to mention the unimportance of the hunt as ritual. Tommy recalls that "when I first took up guiding, didn't no women come here to hunt or fish." He also tells a ribald anecdote about a Chicago doctor and his doxy down for a pretense at fishing. This illustrates the lack of respect for women outside of the civilized norms. Bomar turns a whiskey bottle up to "Argive Helen and all her kin." He refers to the wife of Laus as "his Helen [who] stayed at home making quilts and raising his young." The Chicago doxy bore the name also. Goosetree plans to turn the situation to money with his cabins. When the boy and his guide move into their blind, he notices a litter of cigarette butts, one hardly smoked and smudged with lipstick: "Instinctively the boy averted his gaze." Women have intruded into the male ritual. Much of his initiation is into knowledge of the sexual nature of men and women and the social conduct of it, a duality held into a straining unity, the parts and the whole.

The boy's mother sees him off and makes a feminine mistake about the masculine world. There is a "humiliation of the leave-taking," as he innocently allows her to dress him, as though for Sunday school or a party, in his hunting togs (he is not really entitled to them yet); he soon realizes that "hunters changed for the Lake after they got there." Like the other men in his family, as anecdotes illustrate, he is "hindered by the solicitude of women." Filled with pride at following the same road Laus took to the Lake, he recounts the tales to Bomar, who seems not to know them. The boy parrots his mother's interpretation about the far-distant past. "You might know it would be a long time," Bomar says bitterly. "The United Daughters like'm dead." To the boy's puzzlement,

"I mean all united daughters. The club don't make any difference. In union is strength. That's their battle cry. But hell, boy, you don't know what I'm talking about. . . . What I mean is the only man they'll have any truck with is a dead one. After a certain age, that is."

Bomar makes this out as general feminine nature, but really it is local. Men have crossed race and class lines with such words on their lips. Although the boy still does not understand, a revelation begins through which he reinterprets many things he has known and taken to mean something else, things close to him, his family and their legends. Soon he is confronted with "the truth heretofore hidden in things familiar. . . ." He recalls his grandfather's attacks on the church that really are veiled attacks on things feminine, all the while uttering no explicit word against women. With Uncle Bomar, the boy "felt a difference. Bomar had actual women in mind and a grievance which seemed, however mysterious, real and vaguely threatening." And he knows too his uncle had "inadvertently . . . allowed talk which he considered unseemly to pass between them."

Knowledge of the sexual conflict in society and in men and women is only a start. The initiation is far from complete. The form of the whole the boy comes to before he can comprehend it fully:

> But now that he thought of things in a way he never had thought before, all which touched him dearly lay bright and clear before his vision, the beginning, the middle, and the end clarified in a burst of illumination, where the parts were the whole and the whole defined in parts.

And he gains this "by accident" before he reaches the hunting ground. It is the form of wholeness and perfection, proper to innocence; but it is not real in this world. He misunderstands it, as on the occasion of his first long pants his brother's remark, "Keep 'em buttoned," had a meaning beyond what the boy understood. Just so, the mahogany frame is a form that can take more than one content, that now contains a picture of Laus, but as easily can hold one of Bomar or in time of the boy himself. But the boy's vision is a form without the content of his own experience. A similiar perception of unity comes to him at dawn on the hunt and dawn in his experience:

> Never had he been able so see so clearly and so far. He thought it must be like this with animal eyes at night or whenever they hunt, to see and not know they are seeing, when the vision and prey are made one for the spring.

I regard both of these visions as the ideal truth of innocence, and truth brings strength: "A wonderfully fresh strength streamed through his body. All things seemed at a beginning. It was the world on the first day." However, many things befell the world on subsequent days.

The age-old analogies between a life and the change of the seasons or the course of a day; a journey from one place to another, such as from plain to mountain; the course of the mind's progress from ignorance to illumination, from darkness to light, the soul from its corporeal involvements to the union with God—these are the traditional patterns hovering in the background of the entire story, lending it the strength of time, tradition, and universal metaphor.

The last revelation is the crucial one for the boy. Just as "all things he had found different from his imaginings" at the start of the hunt, and "almost without attending it, so fast did it happen, one certainty after another had slipped away from him," so the revelations had proceeded. He had expected the guides to be "simple, noble men," lean and keen-eyed like the guides of Laus; he found them to be foulmouthed, greedy, and drunken, if competent. Tommy called Bomar "a pretty bastard" in camaraderie rather than insult; his uncle had fought for less. Women had intruded into the hunt in a frivolous way, lessening the high seriousness of it. He mistook a mudhen for a duck. The boy had set out, in the classic pattern of innocence, "never doubting that things could be otherwise than as they seemed." Yet at every step of the way the realities were different from the appearances, the boy learned.

The culmination is Laus. A picture of the family legend has hung in the mahogany frame beside the mantel like a household god, which indeed he is. The boy's mother has held him up as a model. His own words for Laus are highfalutin; no reality corresponds to them. "He's the one that was such a rounder," Bomar says at one point, though it comes out that the uncle has pondered Laus's significance more deeply than that. The picture had never caused the boy to think of his forebear. The picture-man has the marks of mortality all over him; he is simply a man. "Tall, gallant, and forever young," the figure in the boy's mind is beyond human limitations. This image of the idealized Laus is a form with no human contest. The full and unsentimental truth has got to be learned. The revelation came with force at the end of the hunt: "What he saw made him raise his hand, as though for support." Turning, the boy looked into Bomar's eyes: "They were the eyes in the mahogany frame." Since earlier he had examined his uncle's eyes minutely without noticing this similarity, the new insight means a growth in his being and with it a growth in his comprehension. What does he see? That mighty hunter Laus was a man as Bomar is a man, as he himself is now a young man? The boy sees the human qualities in the eyes; he sees man; he sees himself. All have a man's problems. None is exempt. The youth has climbed to a new plateau of maturity.

With this perception, the final stage of the initiation, comes insight into the difficulties of male adulthood as it takes temporal and local forms. What is the new state of being? The modern boy has entered into loss, first of all, where Campbell's primitive youths experienced "a marvel, a source of wonder, well worth the pain and fright of a second birth." [19] But if he has lost, he has gained. The loss is the unreal idealization of childhood; the gain is a human dimension to history and legend. This too is the pattern of doubleness that has recurred throughout his experiences. Doubleness confronts him in regard to sexuality. However imperfectly, society has bound this fundamental duality into a workable unity. The commercial aspect of the modern world exacerbates the difficulty.

The young man must reconcile many dualities on his new level. His knowledge is adult and will guide him in further experience in the adult world. His initiation is archetypal in that all must go through it in some fashion; however, it is limited by the nature of the modern world, which is not traditional but instead committed to the flux of change. There is of course no ritual initiation into profundities. The enveloping action has shown the theme of dualities all the way through; the experiences of the persons in the action proper have con-

[19] *Masks*, p. 89.

veyed the same truth. Artistically, then, "the parts are the whole and the whole defined in parts." [20]

Yet these words which pertain to the boy's innocent vision of wholeness do not correspond to his adult experience. For he has not gained any cultural certainty that will assure him in regard to the doubleness of sex—indeed, the entire "multiplicity of the conflicts of opposites" that is "not chaos but life as we suffer it," as Lytle has elsewhere put it—only some accidental insights into the empirical way it is done. His insight is as much into the problem as into the answer. Laus, the god of his childhood, has been humanized with these very problems. However, he offers as much possibility as ever of being a guide, I think, no longer as one above the moil but now as a fellow man who did what he could with his own imperfect nature. In the realm of experience, the boy's insight into Laus means that he no longer holds that vision of his innocence, the parts being the whole and the whole defined in parts. Such wholeness is ideal and is not possible to adult experience in the modern world.

---

[20] "The Working Novelist and the Mythmaking Process," in *Myth and Myth-making*, ed. Henry A. Murray (New York, 1960), p. 146.

Toward a Dark Shape:
Lytle's "Alchemy" and the Conquest
of the New World

M. E. BRADFORD

"ALCHEMY" IS NOT one of Andrew Lytle's most important fic-
tions. Simplicity and straightforwardness distinguish it from the Ten-
nessean's characteristic work: from a sequence of creations in which
fable, angle of vision, texture, and subject matter modify and reinforce one another in weighted counterpoint. But this sixty-plus page
novella is nonetheless a thing well and carefully made—an extended
trope spun out of known history and filtered through a believable
observer extrapolated from that history. Moreover, it is (when set
over against the aforementioned novels and short stories) an ex-
tremely useful touchstone, an access into the thematic center or
thrust of Mr. Lytle's career.[1]

Like *At the Moon's Inn* (of which it is sequel or prologue),
"Alchemy" is the tale of Spain's American expansion, of the "example of the conquistadors." Indeed, it is impossible to consider the
one work without checking it against the other. Yet a better place
for commencing this reading is Lytle's own criticism, especially
"The Image as a Guide to Meaning in the Historical Novel," "The
Working Novelist and the Mythmaking Process," and certain
splendid review essays.[2] The procedure is one that has been recom-
mended at least indirectly by the novelist himself: ". . . reading is
one way to learn to write." And he has followed his own suggestion,
even to the point of searching out what is paradigmatic of all "mak-

---

[1] I employ the text printed on pages 103–164 in *A Novel, A Novella and Four
Stories* (New York: McDowell, Obolensky, 1958); the first appearance was in
Kenyon Review, 4 (Summer 1942), 273–327. All subsequent citations from "Al-
chemy" are embodied in my text.

[2] Most of these papers are collected in Lytle's *The Hero with the Private Parts*
(Baton Rouge: Louisiana State University Press, 1966).

ing" from his private creative labors.[3] With "myth" or "image" in Lytle's novella I commence.

The title of "Alchemy" is both a description of an action and an allusion to the frame of reference within which that action unfolds in plot. In the person and performance of the alchemist is gathered much of what has made for the world as we have known it since the Renaissance. Ben Jonson, Marlowe, Goethe, Spengler, and Jung were well advised in their focus upon the breed.[4] For it was always an anomaly in the accommodation of Grace with Nature that was feudal Christendom: an ominous anomaly that augured the disruption of that ontologically pious dispensation. The given creation aways rankled in the bosoms of the grimy denizens of ancient laboratories. And the infernal overtones of their activities were not, from the medieval point of view, unfairly connected with a certain crafty fellow well acquainted with flame and sulphur. From alchemy and its halting efforts toward the transformation of dross into precious ore came the spirit of Francis Bacon, the herald of a new era in which mind and will would combine to further the "greater power and glory" of the species: in which the discursive reason shifted shape into a caldron great enough for seething most of the Western World. Add to the figure of the crypto/chemist the metaphoric associations of the westward and upward Peruvian journey (of conquest, enrichment, and death) toward what was foreseen by the journey makers themselves as a demiparadise, and the meaning of this title is completed, the image at the heart of Lytle's novella identified: a searching out and up, by sacrilegious means, toward the condition of a self-anointed godhead. Discovery and possession of the Indies are, therefore, in this narrative *an alchemy in men*, a movement of the spirit forshadowing all else accomplished by certain hispanic gentlemen in the Eldorado of their wicked dreams. Three tropes, all one in meaning, with the shift in

[3] *Ibid.*, p. 20; pp. 178–201. On page 9 of this volume, in the first of the essays referred to in the body of these remarks, Lytle observes of the importance of a governing metaphor or central image "placed at the post of observation and at the historical center of the author's seeing eye" to the organization of good historical fiction: "It was right to begin here, because it is here the author began. His image will not take the final measure of a book, but once it is located there will be less risk of misreading for there will be a common referent."

[4] Lytle read Jung's *Psychology and Alchemy* after the composition of "Alchemy."

space and fortune manifesting an inner and impious outreach toward a condition not available to our mortality.

Hovering just behind the action in "Alchemy" (as he was in *At the Moon's Inn*) is the presence or personage who made possible the just described juxtaposition and melding of spatial and metaphysical overtones, the Admiral of the Ocean Seas, Don Christopher Columbus. The great Italian seaman is the original adventurer in the realms beyond the sunset. Hence he is the moral ancestor of Hernando de Soto, the antagonist in the Spanish novel; as he is of Francisco Pizarro, who plays the same role in Lytle's novella. The narrators in both works act Ishmael to the Ahab of their great captains. But the nameless soldier who speaks in the latter is never so taken up in his expedition's monomania as is Tovar, who painfully learns his way through and out of Florida in the former.[5] Therefore he can, from the first, speak of the Governor General in a language that judges and condemns while it describes; can label Pizarro as a "witch" who "watched the brew of circumstance" among his men so as to "let its smell tell him what to do . . ." (p. 103). And, remembering, he can also render this report in the appropriate frame of reference, connecting the Peruvian march upcountry with a conversation of the "great admiral" himself, words borrowed from an equally anonymous sentinel who had overheard Columbus' forecast of a "Paradise of Pleasure" in the mountains they are climbing (p. 124). But it is in *At the Moon's Inn* that all the conquistadors are morally gathered into their prototype. The episode in which this gathering occurs requires full examination before we turn to an analysis of the design of "Alchemy."

The portion of Lytle's De Soto novel to which I refer comes early (pp. 43–47) in that account of the first white incursion into the Southland and clarifies what is at stake in the hidalgo's decision to find his

[5] *At the Moon's Inn* (Indianapolis: The Bobbs-Merrill Co., 1941). Hereafter, references to this book are indicated in the body of the essay.

Tovar's involvement in De Soto's vainglory facilitates the expansion of his "education" into a full novel. Only when warned by the haughty wanderer's ghost ("the will is not enough") does this loyal liegeman recognize what folly he has performed in questing after an "abiding city" in this sublunary, transient, and imperfectible world (pp. 396–398). The immunity of the narrator in "Alchemy" to the same sick dream makes inevitable that his account be brief. However, the veteran of Columbus' voyages gives a summary quality or depth to his post of observation as does the presence of Tovar and De Soto in Pizarro's band to the former's North American reportage.

own Cuzco and Montezuma. Its scene is a predeparture banquet of De Soto and his lieutenants, a company he has brewed up into a compound suited to the Florida journey. Its principal is, however, one unlike these younger men, an ancient Marshal of Seville, crusader and true knight who serves well as a mouthpiece for the Godsweal of medieval Spain. The old warrior has no horror of bloodshed or long marches. But for his generation military, political, and economic actions were exercises of trust, not means of self-glorification. And they believed in turn that genuine self-realization comes with acceptance of the obligations imposed by a place. Out of that background the Marshal admonishes the young men before him concerning the spiritual unworthiness of the venture they are to commence on the following morning. As he describes his own part in wars against the heathen, details the perils yet confronting the Christian West, and builds to a final (and thoroughly ignored) toast to "that poverty of the Cross which is Spain," he points back to the beginnings of the apostasy he deplores. Columbus is the villain of his discourse, the "alchemist" who "left such a hole in Christendom that . . . it can never be plugged." In the fellowship of "new" men, empire-builders and victims of a secularized eschatology (including priests, noblemen, and his own grandson), this Quixote with a sting is alone. But the remainder of this novel proves him out as wiser than his sullen auditors. Later in *At the Moon's Inn*, in the book's climactic scene, the Adelantado of Florida, Civil and Military Governor of Cuba, and Vice-Regent of God in North America (above Mexico), commits himself to the old enemy whom all alchemists serve, to him who from the first offered full power over and an immunity to the law of Nature.[6] A near general ruin is the issue (pp. 366–374.)[7]

In "Alchemy" we are not shown the final fruit of Pizarro's calculated presumption. But we are taken so far as the moment and place of its consummation, the interlude of silence following the great

[6] For additional evidence of Lytle's preoccupation with modern man's Promethean attitude toward Nature as a target for his will, the reader should consult *The Hero with the Private Parts*, pp. 139, 158, 199, and 201; the "Introduction" to the second edition of *Bedford Forrest and His Critter Company* (New York: McDowell, Obolensky, 1960), pp. x–xvii; "How Many Miles to Babylon," in *Southern Renascence* (Baltimore: Johns Hopkins University Press, 1953), ed. Louis D. Rubin, Jr., and Robert D. Jacobs, pp. 31–34; and *Shenandoah*, 3 (Summer 1952), 30–32, for an untitled Agrarian afterthought.

[7] De Soto's specific sin in this scene is to usurp the authority of his priest.

victory at Caxamalca. Like De Soto, Pizarro cannot finally corrupt himself unless he brings others to share in his undoing. His "brewing" is therefore slow and difficult, even with the record of earlier freebooting expeditions fresh in the memory of his men. Though the Spaniards are still nominally Christian, they are prevented from seeing their enterprise for what it is by the language of religious conflict which was part of the complex baggage they brought with them out of their recent victory over the Moors. This paradox is on the side of their leader, pushing the orthodox in his company toward the anti-miracle of which they speak, once triumphant. Almost every detail that Lytle rearranged, added to, or subtracted from the chronicles he appears to have consulted clarifies the reader's impression of this necromancy and therefore points up the burden of his interiorized retelling of their story.[8] Every page of "Alchemy" builds toward this final and most significant of "inventions." Similarly, each moment contributes to the already described envelope of metaphor surrounding and informing its plot. Both patterns are closed in the same nighttime colloquy.

After foreshadowing (in the "brewer" image) Pizarro's part in the remainder of the novella and marking his cohorts as "ignorant" and "gamblers," Lytle's narrator follows the amazing 177–man "army" from Tumbez and the muggy, infested coastlands (representing the ordinary human condition), across the barren Cordillera, the rich foothill valleys, and the front range of the Andes (signifying the inevitable struggles of the truly ambitious—usually the spiritually ambitious), and finally to the mountain fastness of Atahualpa and the "thing of radiance" (here a travesty of the spiritual, despite the crusader's rhetoric) which they imagine there awaits them (p. 164). But I have earlier identified the role of geography-as-figure in this sequence. It would be unintelligible without the addition of another ingredient to the dialectic of the total work. Just as Lytle uses the countryside of Peru to specify what his "visiting" Spaniards are

[8] The ancient historical documents concerning the Peruvian invasion are well represented in William H. Prescott's *History of the Conquest of Peru* (Boston, 1847). That Lytle knew and used Prescott is evident. Whether he worked back from that composite to its source I cannot say. I have used the Modern Library text of the Brahmin historian which contains the Peruvian study and also his *History of the Conquest of Mexico* (New York: Random House, n.d.).

about, he similarly employs its native inhabitants. And their role in giving significance to the tale is perhaps more important than place conquered or attitude of conquerors.

The Incas are the antitypes of their European adversaries. Indian passivity and absolutism aggravate the white men's assertiveness and individualism—do this even as they spell the empire's doom. The polity and religion of the ancient South Americans are indistinguishable and are centered in the person of their ruler. For that reason there are *no Indians but the Inca*: no one to secure that lord's position but the emperor himself. It is therefore unfortunate for him that he has permitted no initiative to any liegeman, even to his household guard, the Canari. The arrant effrontery of their slaughter in the courtyard disarms Atahualpa (pp. 160–162). In fact, the Inca has so completely swallowed his own rhetoric of deification that he and his minions come almost unarmed into Pizarro's lair. Had he not been so over-confident, the Spaniard would never have been permitted to arrive at that fortification (p. 135). In addition, his natural vanity has been recently strengthened by victory over a rival heir to his father, Huayna Capac. Once Atahualpa is pulled down from the royal chair, his world is dead. That the "moss chins" should have intended this sacrilege from the moment of their landing was as inconceivable to his servants as it was to him. As Renaissance men, the Spaniards are *all will*. The Indians are *all submission*. The proper attitude of the truly human being is, of course, somewhere in between.[9]

The turn in "Alchemy" occurs halfway in Pizarro's march (pp. 131–132). Natural hazards, surprise, puzzlement, and fatigue begin to undermine the morale of his little band. While speaking always "like a man who repeats another's command" (p. 129), the skilled commander offers to release all who would leave to return to a base camp. To these faint hearts he will even reserve a small reward. But to the bold will go a "share" (a token of their active personal seconding of his design) of the "gold" waiting still higher among the peaks. The Gideon-like gesture (along with directions from the Inca's emissaries) removes the last troublesome impurity from Pizarro's

[9] *Ibid.*, pp. 762 and 773. Prescott observes that the monolithic properties of the Peruvian empire damaged the character of its citizens and made it ripe for conquest.

alchemical mixture. The Spaniards who continue to Caxamalca need few orders and no encouragement in the remainder of their journey. Nor do they doubt again—not even when the "dark thing," always in attendance upon the alchemist, steps into the place of the "white robed" object of their desire and receives them into its embrace (p. 164).

Throughout this novella Lytle's narrator is addressing a silent audience, probably an audience of his peers (i.e., other old soldiers). He puts to them an implicit question about the fortune of their generation, especially as it shared in the opening of the New World. He does well (as a storyteller) to reserve his normative denomination of Pizarro until his tale is finished, until the label of "alchemist" is indisputable. For the same reason he is wise to delay the inversion of the novella's religious terminology until De Soto murmurs "miracle," until we have seen the man of God play devil's tool. Verisimilitude requires both procedures. And so does art.

In "Alchemy" a singular segment of Western history—a segment Catholic and full of echoes from the old dispensation—is rendered in a specifically transitional and retrospective context, a context reminiscent of Joseph Conrad's practice with point of view. All of these characteristics gave Andrew Lytle an opportunity to search out the full implications of modernity with an unusual and ironic power: with far more authority and purchase than would have been possible had his scene been recent Northern Europe or North America. Mr. Lytle *found a shape* in the record of Pizarro and his band, an image inclusive of the meaning he had earlier discovered in the Southern experience. His Spanish fiction sheds a powerful refracted light on alchemists closer to home. They and their handiwork have ever been his theme.[10]

---

10 I have not accounted for much of the functional detail of "Alchemy": the ominous preparation by the narrator in his talk of Fortune (p. 109); in his meditation on the Incas' great road as a treadmill (p. 112); in his accounts of the conduct and appearance of the Incas' ambassadors (pp. 120–128). It is enough to say that in each of these details there is reinforcement for the interpretation I have attempted.

The Walls of Mortality

SIDNEY J. LANDMAN

I am unreconciled to what I know,
And I am old with questions never done
That will not let me slumber, Randall, my son.

HOMAGE TO Andrew Nelson Lytle must include recognition of what is surely one of the finest pieces of short fiction to have emerged from the Southern renaissance of the first half of the twentieth century: "Jericho, Jericho, Jericho." This story was first published in the 1936 spring issue of the *Southern Review* upon the invitation of its editors. Since that time it has been anthologized along with the similarly great stories augmenting the rich store to which Faulkner, Porter, Welty, Warren, Taylor and others have contributed.

"Jericho, Jericho, Jericho" is a parable of the fall of the South and a compelling and poignant story of human strength and frailty. Two aspects of Lytle's technique in the story are remarkable, and both of them are manifestations of the point of view from which the story is told. First of all, the third-person-limited point of view is the best possible vehicle for presenting to the reader the portrait of the strong, fearful matriarch, Katherine McCowan (the widow of General Malcolm McCowan), on her deathbed. And secondly, in limiting his narration to the consciousness of a dying human being, Lytle has achieved as successfully as any writer has ever done the *tour de force* of writing about a universal experience which no one has ever lived to describe—the throes of death. "The Bishop Orders His Tomb in Saint Praxed's Church," "An Occurrence at Owl Creek Bridge," the "Benjy" section of *The Sound and the Fury*, and "The Jilting of Granny Weatherall" all present psychic states and conditions which the typical reader cannot know unless he is mentally defective or until he dies. Such preternatural circumstances give the imaginative artist a free hand in exploring this realm of human experience, and its literary representation may be both terrifying and lyrical. Lytle's achievement in this kind is unsurpassed in literature.

"Jericho, Jericho, Jericho" is set near Madison, Alabama, some time around 1930. The McCowan plantation is made up of four thousand of the richest acres in Long Gourd Valley and takes its name from that valley. With the clipped beginning sentence, "She opened her eyes," quite as memorable as "Nobody knew the color of the sky," the reader is plunged into the psyche of the eighty-seven-year-old woman who has had summoned to her bedside her grandson, in whom her hopes for the future of her world repose. From the dying unconscious well of her remaining cerebration comes Biblical justification for Kate McCowan's *modus operandi* in life, her very *raison d'être*. She has been Joshua, savior, leader, and preserver of her "people"—plantation personnel as well as family—directing their secure establishment upon the land, the only source of earthly comfort and strength. And now there remains the final task of transmitting this charge, until now the responsibility of this woman long since widowed, bereft of the usual son to assume the mantle, and left only with the grandson, Richard McCowan, the son of a "foolish" mother who seems not to realize that "it takes a heap more than pants to make a man." "He looked a little like his grandpa, but somehow there was something missing. . . ." And yet Miss Kate is filled with pity and love too; for Dick is "mighty young and helpless and ignorant," and this naiveté and colossal unknowing of what the future holds in store for him endears him to her all the more.

Dick has brought with him to see his grandmother die, as she knows full well, his intended bride, Eva Callahan, suggestively named after that archetypal corrupter of man. Lytle's description of Eva as Miss Kate sees her suggests also Rossetti's primordial Lilith:

> so went
> Thy spell through him, and left his straight neck bent,
> And round his heart one strangling golden hair.

Mrs. McCowan observes that Eva's "heavy hair crawled about her neck to tangle the poor, foolish boy in its ropes." Even so, she tries to soften the gauche presence of the young couple with her characteristic *esprit*: "There an't nothing strange about dying. But I an't in such an all-fired hurry. I've got a heap to tell you about before I go." Kate's further inquiries into Eva's origins, her attempts to derive her from the Callahans of the Goosepad community, soon reveal that Eva is a city gal from Birmingham, an upstart industrial town ("I've got a mule older'n Birmingham"), and that she is not allied to that which is traditional in Southern life and therefore could not possibly appreciate the real value of the land her prospective husband will inherit or the way of life that subsistence upon it entails. Like Peter Taylor's Miss Leonora, Kate McCowan sees human relationships not in a romantic light, but in terms of dynastic and communal good. Were Dick sensible enough to choose as a wife one of the Carlisle girls, the dowry of land she would bring would give Miss Kate a landing on the river for Long Gourd. The gorgeous Eva will wrinkle up on Dick, but "the only wrinkles land gets can be smoothed out by the harrow."

Miss Kate's dynastic consciousness is further lacerated as she examines Eva's small waist, which is not wholesomely suited to childbearing. But the crushing realization begins to dawn on the old woman that Dick is a romantic; he is not interested in propagating the McCowans on the McCowan plantation; he does not realize that most young women are the same when viewed as objects of husbandly affection and that more practical considerations than mere romanticized personal preference must form the basis for choosing the new chatelaine of Long Gourd. Nor does Eva comport with Mrs. McCowan's notion of a proper young lady in allowing Dick to ascertain that she does not wear a corset.

Already too much brainwashed by Eva's modern sense of values and too much an apostate from the traditional sense of "family" and paternal responsibility to even its remoter, dead, and unborn members, Dick indicates to his grandmother that the inheritors of her plantation will not continue to care for poor old "tetched" cousin George, who, in the fashion of Uncle Toby, rehearses his Confederate cavalry charges out in the yard at night. Rather, they will hire a professional keeper for him while they live mostly in town. So it is with greater intensity that Mrs. McCowan realizes that she must do something about Long Gourd, about Eva, that the slut must not eat it up. But she is as ineffectual as the mother in Donald Davidson's "Randall, My Son" (the source of my epigraph), who unwillingly surrenders to the realities of the intrusion of the new order upon her private world and the world of the South as both are symbolized by her son's failure to cherish and cultivate his inherited land. "Jericho, Jericho, Jericho" (at this level) and "Randall, My Son" are both emblems of the failure of the traditional values of the old South and serve as measures of the new South. Katharine McCowan takes a giant stride toward the burial ground when she realizes that there will not always be a Long Gourd nor always a McCowan on it. Katharine McCowan, with her failing consciousness, embodies the falling order of Southern culture: in a sense, she *is* the South.

Apart from her symbolic value and the excellent technique used to present her point of view, Kate is a remarkable personality in her own right. She is one of the dominating, wise old women who people the pages of Southern fiction over and over again in Taylor, Welty, Porter, Lytle (in other stories such as "Mister McGregor" and "Old Scratch in the Valley"), and especially in Faulkner's women whose rule of life is illustrated in his fiction with amplitude:

> I think that as fine an influence as any young man can have is one reasonable old woman to listen to . . . because they are much more sensible than men, they have to be. They have held families together and it's because of families a race is continued.
>
> (*Faulkner at Nagano*, p. 70)

These women are literally drawn from the life of the South.

As random experiences from the broad panorama of her life surface in her dying mind, the personality and outstanding qualities of Miss Kate in all her strength and weakness become clear. A kindly, genuine, loving concern for people in all stations of life and in all relations to her in her world has enabled this remarkable woman to build and maintain the miracle of Long Gourd. To Negro slaves in her youth and to Negro servants in her adult years she is firm but protective and loving: "You, Ants, where's my stick? I'm a great mind to break it over your trifling back." And her private bedside conference with Dick must be well lighted:

Throw open them blinds, Ants.
. . . .
You don't have to close the door so all-fired soft. Close it natu-
rally. And you can tip about all you want to later. I won't be
hurried to the burying ground. And keep your head away from
that door. What I've got to say to your new master is private.

She knows that Ants is an eavesdropper, but she loves him just the
same. The affection is reciprocated: "Listen at you, mistiss." And her
dynastic care of the people on the Long Gourd is amusingly and painfully illustrated in her apprehension of the Snopesian bushwhackers
(in better days barn-burners) who menace and try to tamper with
her Negroes. There is the youthful affection for her husband, Malcolm, so long ago and before so much trouble came; her compassion
and love for her poor brother Jack with his cleft palate and propensity
to drink, cut in two by a chain shot when Breckinridge charged at
Murfreesboro; her dying concern for Cousin George—all evidences
of the strands of love and softness twisted with the steel. Old Mrs.
Penter Matchem thought a whip could do anything. Kate knows it
cannot.

Miss Kate's fine sense of humor, a saving grace for a strong woman
of any sort, is evident in her relations with Ants; in her knowing herself really to be an old hag, not the beautiful lady that her grandson
Dick is calling her as he sits on the edge of her bed; in her comical
proof of the dangers of small waists, instanced to Dick to sour him on
Eva, from the histories of the daughters of old Mrs. Penter Matchem
(herself provocatively named)—the one dying from affected bowels
so tight was her lacing, the other being childless for the same reason;
in her final comment to Dick about Eva, "I suppose the safest place
for a man to take his folly is to bed"; and finally in the last touch
of grim irony as she lies dying, contemplating her sins: "She'd be
damned if she would go until she was ready to go. She'd be damned
all right, and she smiled at the meaning the word took on now."

Katharine McCowan is every inch a king:

The boy leaned over and touched her gently. "Not even death
would dispute you here, on Long Gourd, Mammy."

But the suffering and struggle and tribulation have earned her authority with a corresponding hardness, as Dick learns when he sug-

gests that no respectable woman asks a young gentleman how he knows that his affianced wears no corset: "I'm not a respectable woman. No woman can be respectable and run four thousand acres of land." And the confrontation years earlier with the bushwhackers: "You'd shoot a woman quicker because she has the name of being frail. Well, I'm not frail, and my Navy Six ain't frail." Tempering this authoritarian, almost unattractive though comical, unfeminine hardness is a practical and sweet reasonableness: "Everybody has a time to die, and I'll have no maudlin nonsense about mine."

Yet these details do not round out the image. There is finally in Mrs. McCowan's nature a redeeming frailty of conscience, a sense of guilt for the one damning error of her life. There were times when the enormous ancestral bed was "not wide enough for her nor long enough when her conscience scorched the cool wrinkles in the sheets." The charming naiveté and vast ignorance of life in the young grandson is a "quenching drink to a sin-thirsty old woman." But the torturing ambiguity inherent in that one thing she had done, enlarging Long Gourd by paying the taxes on the land of a dead neighbor (possibly a kinsman) whose pusillanimous son-in-law could not even muster the tax money for his own farm in Madison, much less for that of his wife's dowry—that ambiguity never really leaves her alone. Mrs. McCowan had promised Iva Louise's father that his land, the sacramental value of which he realized as fully as Mrs. McCowan did, would not be squandered; and under Mrs. McCowan's management it had not been. Perhps she did the right thing for the wrong reason—perhaps followed an innate acquisitiveness and thus compromised means to a nobler end, the sacramental preservation of land. And after so doing, after assuming an essentially masculine and aggressive role in this act, her tenderer feminine conscience presses her down with the dubiety of her deed. Kate McCowan's personality is a combination of human weaknesses and very great strengths; it is dominant and intense, and admirable for its courage.

The consummate style of "Jericho, Jericho, Jericho" is manifest in a variety of qualities; the assured, natural, easy narrative flow of language, the sure ear for cadences of speech and Southern patois. It is remarkably expressed in seven agrarian similes which not only adorn the story but thematically link the character of Kate McCowan to its action. The narrative begins as Miss Kate awakens from a sleep that seems unusually long to her, having pulled her floating psyche, as it were, under the covers: "And now she was resting, clear-headed and quiet, her thoughts clicking like a new-greased mower." The menaces of Eva to Dick and to Long Gourd Miss Kate forcibly communicates to her grandson: "You won't be free much longer—the way she looks at you like a hungry hound." As Dick goes out, "She watched the door close quietly on his neat square back. Her head whirled and turned like a flying jennet." And after comes the rigorous remembrance of the one thing she did. "Suddenly, like the popping of a thread in a loom, the struggles of the flesh stopped, and the years backed up and covered her thoughts like the spring freshet she had seen so many times creep over the dark soil." Finally at the end, "How exquisite the sound, like a bell swinging without ringing. Suddenly it came to her. She was dying. . . . Her will left her. Life withdrawing gathered like a frosty dew on her skin."

The most skillful technical and stylistic ingredient of "Jericho" is the portrayal of the hastening of death and of Miss Kate's physical and psychical extinction with its train of disordered thought patterns and progressive dredging up of experience from an earlier and earlier past. Emerging from her long and deep sleep at the beginning of the story, her consciousness almost poetically chanting, "forever she had floated above the counterpane; between the tester and the counterpane she had floated . . . her eyes, as apart from her as the mirror on the bureau, rested upon the half tester. . . ." Dick's presence (Dick is now twenty-six years of age) conjures the fond recollection of a boy:

> Whom she had diapered a hundred times and had washed as he stood before the fire in the round tin tub, his little back swayed and his little belly sticking out in front, rosy from the scrubbing he had gotten. *Mammy, what for I've got a hole in my stummick; what for, Mammy?*

But a part of Miss Kate's mind is still working very efficiently with the current problems of Long Gourd, the solutions merely being deferred until she may rise from her sickbed. Ants has to be shooed out and told not to eavesdrop, but momentarily he must be stopped:

No, wait. I had something else on my mind—what is it? Yes,

how many hens has Melissy set? You don't know. Find out. A few of the old hens ought to be setting. Tell her to be careful to turn the turkey eggs every day. No, you bring them and set them under my bed. I'll make sure. We got a mighty pore hatch last year.

Backward and forward in time her mind moves, with a sharpening intensity of sensory experiences, odors, sights, sounds, textures:

Sweeping over the mounds of her body rising beneath the quilts came the old familiar odors—the damp, strong, penetrating smell of new-turned ground; the rank, clinging, resistless odor of green-picked feathers stuffed in a pillow by Guinea Nell, thirty-odd years ago; tobacco on the mantel, clean and sharp like smelling salts; her father's sweat, sweet like stale oil; the powerful ammonia of manure turned over in a stall; curing hay in the wind; the polecat's stink on the night air, almost pleasant, a sort of commingled scent of all the animals, man and beast; the dry smell of dust under a rug; the over-strong scent of too-sweet fruit trees blooming; the inhospitable wet ashes of a dead fire in a poor white's cabin; black Rebecca in the kitchen; a wet hound steaming before a fire. There were other odors she could not identify, overwhelming her, making her weak, taking her body and drawing out of it a choking longing to hover over all that she must leave, the animals, the fences, the crops growing in the fields, the houses, the people in them. . . .

The clarity of past experiences engulfs Miss Kate painfully and sweetly:

Brother Jack stood before her, handsome and shy, but ruined from his cradle by a cleft palate, until he came to live only in the fire of spirits. And she understood, so clear was life down to the smallest things. She had often heard tell of this clarity that took a body whose time was spending on the earth.

But the news of Jack's death had come; she had sat up all that night, and "she had seen that night as if she had been on the field, the parties moving over the dark field hunting the wounded and dead . . . all the while relief parties, moving, blots of night, sullenly moving in the viscous blackness." And now death was coming for her, hunting her down:

There was some mistake, some cruel blunder; for there now,

tipping about the carpet, hunting in her wardrobe, under the bed, blowing down the fire to its ashes until they glowed in their dryness, stalked the burial parties.

Then the thought comes that first she must do something about Long Gourd. Or was it too late? Lytle concludes the story with the final death-throe, which echoes but in no way yields to Granny Weatherall's bumping, knocking cart and blue pinpoint of light:

> There was a roaring; the wind blew through her head once, and a great cotton field bent before it, growing and spreading, the bolls swelling as big as cotton sacks and bursting white as thunderheads. From a distance, out of the far end of the field, under a sky so blue that it was painful-bright, voices came singing, *Joshua fit the battle of Jericho, Jericho, Jericho—Joshua fit the battle of Jericho, and the walls come a-tumbling down.*

The ironic reversal of the Biblical prototype of this story is thus completed in its conclusion; for just as Kate McCowan is in life a Joshua establishing and perpetuating his people on chosen and hallowed ground, so in death is she defeated and metamorphosed into Jericho, the object of Joshua's destruction. The final irony comes in the voice of defeat and destruction from the unwitting Negro field hands singing from a happier and more vigorous and hopeful past in the life of her native South, and in her own life, singing of the final reality. Indeed, "Jericho, Jericho, Jericho" is a story of death: a recognition, a mourning, and a tribute.

Andrew Lytle's Selva Oscura

BREWSTER GHISELIN

CLEAR THOUGH it is in conceptual design, the thought of Andrew Lytle cannot be grasped in its substance except through penetration to its intuitive ground, a sensibility matured in the communion of humanity and manifested in the communications of the story-teller and commentator. In the movements of consciousness and life thus inclined and enlarged the thought is given objects, shape, and emphasis. The order so attained bespeaks the essence that issued it. Complete disclosure is achieved through the artist's imaginative mastery of his one subject: man concretely existent and active, in his animal and spiritual duality—in his primitive wholeness of passion and his passionate aspiration toward an order sustaining his being and realizing his humanity.

The dominant condition of mankind represented in Mr. Lytle's fiction and examined in his essays is a dark predicament, that of our own time, though of long preparation in the heart and the world and therefore manifest also in the past: the condition of human life confused and diminished under the dispensations of a world primarily secular. A single illustration of his view of that disastrous conditon will display its essentials. Both what it is and what it entails appears in the novella *Alchemy* when at the glorious culmination of the bloody conquest of Incan gold, undertaken by the Spanish in pretense of bringing Christianity to the Indians and in its consummation miscalled by them "God's miracle," the narrator expresses his sense of its true nature: "As they reached out their hands to clasp their desires, that other—the dark thing—stepped forward to receive them."

Such is Andrew Lytle's vision of the nature of human action when

73

the passions that call it forth and direct it are spent in unregulated liberty. Indulgence of unlimited will or of uninhibited appetite, without regard for any measure recognized in the heart or authorized by it in the world, is a mechanical and inordinate process, endless except in the psychic arrest of debility or in physical death. In Lytle's first novel, *The Long Night*, the consequences of that process, exemplified in Pleasant McIvor's pursuit of his father's murderers and his secret execution of them, are less conclusive than in his later writing. For McIvor's course is modified when, pursuing his victims into the Confederate army, he discovers the communion of comradeship in war. He slackens in his purpose, delays, but does not desist until after it has brought about the death of his one true friend, and his power to complete his vengeance is lost through the exhaustion of his will. Then seeing his utter desolation he retreats from the world into the mountains. But though he marries and rears a family there, he is never truly restored, either to the community of man or, in the depths of his nature, to himself: he cannot dispel the darkness he has drawn about him.

In all Lytle's subsequent fiction those characters whose abandonment of measure submits them to compulsive process, whether predominantly of the ego or of the instinctual nature, come unequivocally to the same deprivation and alienation: in the end, they possess neither the fruits of the earth nor any object of love. Their degeneration shows first, and at the same time declares its true nature, in their neglect of these treasures, as in the closely parallel actions of Hernando de Soto and Henry Brent, protagonists respectively of *At the Moon's Inn* and *A Name for Evil*. De Soto refuses his wife's plea that he remain in Spain to settle on the land and bring it to fruition, in order to fulfill the companionship of love that they foresaw in youth. Henry Brent gives his effort mainly to restoration of his decayed ancestral mansion and leaves his fields almost wholly to his hired man and the ruined garden to his wife. Both men in their preoccupation with ambitious designs withdraw their vital attention and support from their wives, and each in a moment of the woman's despair forces upon her his merely sensual passion, a blasting travesty of the love that has failed in him.

The ravisher, in a violence made possible only by loss of his wholeness of sensibility, tries to exact by will what grace alone can give. His action is expression rather than cause of his isolation and disorientation. It is a characteristic incident in that reckless self-indulgence which Lytle has called, in reference to the main action of *At the Moon's Inn*, the "dance of death." Leading that compulsive dance, De Soto goes to the symbolic West to ravage the earth and its people and to destroy himself in a ruthless and fruitless search for gold. Henry Brent brings his wife at last to a place equally delusive and fatal, the garden made beautiful to his eyes and to his paralyzed sensibility by icy winter's effacement of time's marks of imperfection. Both men, through strictly subordinating their inner life and the world around them to demands of the willful ego, bring mortal disaster upon themselves and others.

As Lytle himself has indicated in a letter written during his composition of *At the Moon's Inn*, the obverse of that reductive disorder of the will, of reckless and insatiable ego, is the equally deathly sensuality exemplified in the fate of Nuño de Tovar, follower of De Soto to Florida. Allured by delusions of fulfillment in "an earthly paradise," Tovar "loses . . . everything but attention to the senses." As if he had found the untrammeled innocence of Eden, he gives himself to passionate indulgence. In a dreamlike encounter in the night-black labyrinth of Cuban jungle, he becomes the lover of De Soto's ward Leonora de Bobadilla, marries his mistress only after her pregnancy brings him to disgrace, and goes on to further and darker adventures in Florida. When in the forests of the continent he lives an adulterous idyll with an Indian girl of the wind clan, then weds her in the Indian mode, it is as if his lust embraces the wind. The sensuality that at first "had seemed so simple and innocent" shows itself in its real simplicity as blasting and exhausting, "only feeling and darkness, feeling in darkness, pure and sharp, disembodied as a flame, drawing and consuming the flesh like dry dead wood until of itself it went out, spent by its own fury." Sheer indulgence of the senses is not the way of innocence but of regression, bringing a reduction of consciousness and being, not relief from responsibility and the visitations of judgment, but desolation. The measure of Tovar's offenses seems to be given when, pausing between the play of his sword and his lance in battle, he drinks the water of a pool that flows also with the blood of slaughter, as if he drank the open wound of Christ.

A process so dire in its consequences could hardly begin, certainly could not continue long, but in self-deception—something of little difficulty for humankind, inveterate and confident as we are in self-justification. So it is with the Spanish despoilers putting the New World to the sword, as depicted in *Alchemy* and *At the Moon's Inn*, and with the woodsman Beverly Cropleigh in *The Velvet Horn*, explaining his avoidance of family responsibility as a retreat from the evil of the world, to "live with the beasts," to "begin at the beginning and know the pure image of divinity imprisoned in the darkness of nature."

The true character of Beverly's adventure, as of Tovar's, is indicated in Lytle's remark in his essay "The Son of Man: He Will Prevail": "The forest, mythologically considered, is the realm of the soul entangled in nature's maze." In *The Velvet Horn*, the consequences of that entanglement are intimated in the figure of man clothed in the hide of the beasts he lives with. Though Beverly says, in praise of the plenty he enjoys in the wilderness, "The summer doe gives me her hide," his gain has deprived him of much. The reality of his condition is suggested in the statement that "the hide he wore fitted his body like an outer skin, as beneath it his muscles, with the slightest ripple, moved in a graft of himself to his animal apparel." The same meaning shows unequivocally in the figure of his brother Duncan, also a hunter devoted to the forest, dancing wildly while "the tight fawn pants, the brocaded waistcoat rippled over his muscles." The pun that yields the word *faun*—creature sometimes half goat and half man—draws the forest about that image and strips it to nakedness. And as, a few phrases later, we read "half man, half beast, the dancer now threaded the maze," the sense of a loss of humanity in regression is confirmed and darkened.

Such is the climax, formally figured, of that surrender which for Duncan, and for his sister Julia, began in the forest adventures of childish play, with a sense of sweet disburdenment, delight in the savor of infinitely permissive freedom, as of primordial innocence that knows no evil and can do none. That condition of shadowless joy is possible only to the wholly innocent, and therefore is available to no man or woman. The deception that made possible its continuance—briefly and only as delusion—was a doeskin hunting dress fabricated by Duncan to be worn by his sister, a tailor-made skin, fitting the body close. Symbolically transparent, since it both concealed and revealed, it was a fair image of total nakedness: the livery of Eve serving in Duncan's Eden, without shame (because her nakedness was covered), without denial (because her nakedness was accessible—actually to the eye that images and knows, and potentially to the body that possesses).

In Paradise *any* clothing is a straitjacket, and it denies the freedom of Paradise until it is discarded. So the doeskin dress must be made after a fashion that will impel its throwing off. Tailored with all the cunning of the roused soul, it turns out to be too tight; for it has to be a skin, and therefore to be the same size as the actual skin it must substitute for. The body already fitted in its perfect jacket cannot take another of the same perfection. The other, a deception and inhibition, is intolerable to Duncan's desire and physically intolerable to Julia. Shortly it is rejected for the reality it figured and anticipated—the nakedness of a woman in the real world. What it meant to the brother who made it is revealed, and what it implied—incest, a denial of the division of the male and female aspects of the one flesh—is consummated. In that exposure the return to Paradise is seen for what it is: denial of the differentiations of the real world, withdrawal before the challenge of mature experience, rejection of the soul's advance in the open world—in short, self-deprivation through avoidance of life.

Any treatment of Lytle's fiction in the wholeness of its purport must give more than a little attention to *The Velvet Horn*, that great novel—his latest and finest—in which his vision is consummate in its entirety. In the life-determined fate of the young Lucius, hero of that book, is exemplified the human completeness of attainment that such men as Beverly, Duncan, and Tovar or De Soto and Henry Brent miss. Lucius, a boy, becomes a man through seeing and embracing the necessity of manhood, which must in intuitive awareness of need and in deliberate courage create within the self and assert in the world an order satisfying the whole being. Unlike the sharecroppers who "felt no more responsibility than the sun or weather for what went on" and who "left to themselves . . . would make a truce with nature, grow only the day's need, let the rest of the farm return to the wilderness," Lucius takes the earth and its fruits into his care; he marries the woman who will bear his child engendered in the paradisal wilderness; and, rejecting the allurement of the West which draws him with promise of relief from the incertitudes of his situation in the world, he assumes his place among men and on the land, and there builds his house of lumber sawn from one felled tree, greatest of the grove, that had long been abandoned to decay.

As Lucius discovers, though the gifts of grace come without effort, they are not kept in the same way. Love for the actual earth, of fields and forests, arises as spontaneously as love for a woman, but neither love is secure or complete apart from man's assumption of his responsibility for the integrity of his inmost life and for the order sustaining it in the natural and human world in which he lives.

Neither flight from the world nor conquest of it will serve. For—as all Lytle's work shows—the one course submits life to the guidance of sheer instinct, while subjecting it to the corruptions of the inevitably invading world, and the other can proceed only through endless expediency, in disregard of scruples and prohibitions that would otherwise deflect or end it. Since it is the senses and the ego that are so served and satisfied, these come to rule the lives in which they predominate. And thus is tainted or destroyed the natural good that flows from the abundance of the earth and the heart. The experience of Lucius in *The Velvet Horn* displays the converse of that disaster, fulfillment achieved through creation and preservation of that order which can alone gather the multiplicity of the natural and the fabricated elements of human existence into their unity, instant by instant renewed, in the living flesh of the hero.

There is no tolerable alternative. Inasmuch as any violation of integrity entails a diminution of being, it constitutes a turning away from life in its wholeness. Though the modes of that retreat differ, their ends are one: the Garden, but run wild—the earthly paradise or the Paradise of Pleasure, the precincts of disorder enjoyed in brief and illusory transcendence of the hard conditions of reality. In the work of Andrew Lytle the image is often beautiful and always, essentially, of death: the frozen garden of *A Name for Evil*, the green retreat of Atahualpa in the high Andes, the dark forest.

The Local Universality
of Andrew Lytle*

ALLEN TATE

In Andrew Lytle we have a writer of great versatility who works
so slowly that in the thirty years** since his first novel, *The Long
Night*, was published, only three full-length pieces of fiction have
appeared: *At the Moon's Inn* (1941), *A Name for Evil* (1947), and
The Velvet Horn (1957)—four novels in thirty years, or one every
seven and a half years. That, of course, is not quite the whole story.
His first book, *Bedford Forrest and His Critter Company*, a biography, came out in 1931, and it must be linked with the novels because
it gave Mr. Lytle the opportunity to study the rural life of Tennessee
in its development from frontier to plantation; and the society of
Middle Tennessee from the end of the eighteenth century to its destruction in the Civil War has given him the enveloping action of all
his fiction. Here was a once rooted society uprooted but still living,
if not on the land yet near it, and conscious of its past, as only societies
that have been dislocated by war and defeat can be. His problem as
a novelist has been to discover in his native *milieu* typical actions (he
calls them mythical or archetypal) that permit him to write, not historical novels but novels as history. *Gone With the Wind* is an historical novel; Caroline Gordon's *None Shall Look Back*, Katherine
Anne Porter's *The Old Order*, and Andrew Lytle's *The Velvet Horn*
are fiction as history. This use of history as the source or matrix of
typical actions is not unlike the "history" floating in the background
of *Oedipus Rex* and *Oedipus at Colonus*. The action takes shape out

---

* This essay appeared first as the "Foreword" to *The Hero with the Private
Parts* (Baton Rouge, 1966). Reprinted by permission of the L.S.U. Press.
** This was written in 1965. It is now thirty-eight years since Lytle's *The
Long Night* appeared.

of a vast and turbulent cloud of events, as the funnel of a tornado suddenly forms and descends.

The essays of Andrew Lytle are not like any other literary criticism of our time. He is a professional novelist, but he is not a professional critic. The late R. P. Blackmur years ago defined criticism as the "passionate discourse of an amateur," a kind of discourse which even the exclusively critical writer can never make into an exact science. By "amateur" I take Blackmur to have meant the man *devoted* to the object of his attention—literature, in this case—the man whose developing awareness and possession of the imaginative object becomes in the end self-knowledge. The practicing novelist who sets forth this awareness of his own art has something to say about the art of the novel that even the best professional critics cannot know. Flaubert's letters to George Sand give us fragmentary insights into his search for the precise method necessary to the writing of *Madame Bovary*; yet Flaubert never had time to make a formal attack, in formal essays, upon his central problem, which is the problem that engages every novelist: what techniques will first reveal the subject and then render it most fully? When the novelist tries to tell us *how* he did something he may succeed more fully than his critic in telling us *what* he did; we observe him at his unavoidable task of trial-and-error in developing a technique, or a combination of techniques, that will dissipate the luminous blur of his inchoate subject and bring it into focus.

Lytle's passionate discourse as an amateur is, first, before it gets on the page, a way of talking to himself about what he has found in other novelists who have been useful to him; but once he starts writing out what he has found useful he begins to impart it to the general reader who is standing over his shoulder. But I am not sure that he ever has, in his essays, the general reader before him as a person to whom he feels responsible; and this is as it should be. The kind of high programmatic criticism that we find in these essays is "creative" (if I may use an obsolescent word) in a formal sense similar to that which we find in his best fiction, notably *The Velvet Horn* and *A Name for Evil*. For reading is translation. The essays are close translations of works which Lytle has read, reread, read once again, so that his last reading assumes so complete a mastery of the text that he no longer needs to refer to it. This sentence is his modest declaration of purpose for his critical writing: "It is part of the author's discipline to read well, and to read well you must write it down." The deceptive simplicity of this statement need not mislead us into supposing that writing it down means making casual notes for his own future use. Writing it down here means a formal effort of the imagination which places the writer inside the consciousness of Stephen Crane, Flaubert, Faulkner, Tolstoy; and, in the case of his *The Velvet Horn*, the "post of observation" that he himself after wandering in his *selva oscura* at last knew was the right stance for the work in hand. I cannot think of another record of a novelist's ordeal in the discovery of his technique in the subject which so convincingly reveals the creative process; and it might be more precise to say that "The Working Novelist and the Mythmaking Process" shows us how long meditation on the subject makes it possible for the subject to reveal to the novelist the right techniques for his particular purpose. For Lytle knows better than any writer today that there are no abstract techniques that can be taken down from the shelf, or provided by a computer, and superimposed upon the materials of fiction.

A comparison of Lytle's essays with the *Prefaces* of Henry James will reveal more similarities than differences. The essays and the *Prefaces* are examples of a critical *genre* that Poe invented in "The Philosophy of Composition." The *genre* even after a hundred years has not been given a name which would distinguish it from the various kinds of historical criticism, or of formal criticism, although it has aims in common with both the historical and the formal critical imaginations. The novelist writing about how he wrote is an historian: he tries to reproduce the conditions under which he wrote his novel— conditions which extend from the desk where he is writing out into the vast *mythos* of the social *milieu* of which the finished novel that he is reflecting upon is the formal concentration. When he begins to consider how the formal concentration became possible, he moves into formal criticism. The most brilliant example of this formalistic-historical criticism that I know is Lytle's "The Working Novelist and the Mythmaking Process," an essay from which contemporary novelists may learn a good deal more than James offers them in the *Prefaces*. This is not to say that the *Prefaces* have ceased to have value for us, or that they are not still the greatest criticism of fiction ever written. When James tells us *how* he wrote *The Ambassadors,* his problem was simpler than that of the novelist of the mid-twentieth century. He knew in advance what his enveloping action had to be: the Newsome-Pocock *ethos* in collision with, to them, the mysterious rituals of a society represented by Madame de Vionnet. James's social *milieu* was given, whereas the novelist today must discover his, in that dual process which imposes upon him the ordeal of finding his techniques in the subject. But James had only to locate his post of observation—a task sufficiently difficult—in order to dramatize the values in the conflict of the two cultures.

To the modern novelist the *milieu* is not given; he must discover it, in so far as it will stand still long enough for him to discern in it a form. The advantage enjoyed by Southern novelists since the First World War has consisted in their sense of a vanishing society about to be replaced by a new order the lineaments of which remain indistinct. What the old society was, before it began to disappear, is disputable. The "legend" of the South, like the immense *praxis* of the legend of Oedipus, was there for writers of genius to reduce to a great variety of forms: Faulkner, Porter, Gordon, Young, Warren, and Lytle, all began with the legend, in varying degrees of awareness of it, for it was the given thing to which there was no alternative. Eudora Welty, a writer who seems to have little or no awareness of the Southern legend, is nevertheless looking away from it; for the "heroine" of "Why I Live at the P. O." is a displaced person who has never been away from home and who suffers from lack of her proper place in a society that no longer places people. (This is the plight of the numerous eccentrics of Southern fiction.)

Andrew Lytle's acute sense of the inchoate flux of history out of which the fictional work of art emerges has enabled him to write the most illuminating essays that I have read on *Madame Bovary,* "The Open Boat," and *War and Peace.* This last essay, "The Image as Guide to Meaning in the Historical Novel," successfully refutes Percy Lubbock's view that *War and Peace* is two novels; for he demonstrates the organic relation of the Russian society of that age to the irruption of war, whereas Lubbock saw the novel as unrelated alternations of battles and domestic scenes. Lytle's three essays on William Faulkner are the most searching examination of this writer that we have had;

they will have to be reckoned with by all future critics; for Lytle not only reads the novels, he knows what the novels are written about, what Faulkner's problem was when he confronted his huge enveloping action and set about isolating its typical features. Lytle's commentary on Hemingway, "*A Moveable Feast*: The Going to and Fro," gives us an entirely new insight into Hemingway's limitations. The malice towards his contemporaries back in the twenties Lytle sees as a result of his isolation as a Displaced Person who must hate because he lacks the security of place that would permit him to love.

It may be said in summary that Andrew Lytle brings to the analysis of works by other writers the same insight that enables him to write about his own. He writes about *Madame Bovary* as if he had written Flaubert's masterpiece. This criticism is entirely original: Lytle is not interested in what the professional critics have written about Tolstoy, Flaubert, and Faulkner; it is not a proliferation of other criticism. And it is universal criticism that takes its stance in a particular place at a particular time.

Yankees of the Race: The Decline and Fall of Hernando de Soto*

ROBERT G. BENSON

Yis, Werld, and ther-to here myn honde,
To forsake God and hys seruyse.
(The Castle of Perseverance)

ANDREW LYTLE TAKES a dark view of the early European ventures in the New World; and his second novel, *At the Moon's Inn*, which chronicles the ill-fated Florida expedition of Hernando de Soto, is an *exemplum* dramatizing the failure of that Satanic self-assertion which characterized such ventures. While working on the novel (first published in 1941), Mr. Lytle described the central action in a letter to D. L. Chambers:

> Under the influence of gold, that is the materialistic view of the world, the mind of Christendom, and its spirit, sets out on its dance of death. The small army will have all the forms of its chivalry, but it is not seeking to deliver the Holy Sepulchre from the hands of the infidels. It is seeking the essence of materialism, its own spiritual destruction.[1]

The main characters in the novel are De Soto and Tovar, originally De Soto's second in command, but demoted before the expedition reaches Florida for fathering a child on one of the ladies attending De Soto's wife. As M. E. Bradford has already noted, the principal thematic concerns of *At the Moon's Inn* are the same as those of

* This essay appeared in a slightly different form under the title "The Progress of Hernando de Soto in Andrew Lytle's *At the Moon's Inn*" in *The Georgia Review*, 27 (1973), 232–244.
1 This letter and another concerning *At the Moon's Inn* are quoted by Noel Polk, "Andrew Nelson Lytle: A Bibliography of His Writings," *Mississippi Quarterly*, 23 (Fall 1970), 453–457. An updated version of this bibliography is included in this volume.

"Alchemy," Mr. Lytle's novella on the Peruvian conquest.[2] In both works, the action condemns the human striving "by sacrilegious means, toward the condition of self-anointed godhead" (Bradford, p.58, this volume). Predictably, the treatment of this theme is fuller and more complex in the novel; the self-glorification and the ultimate rejection of God are more elaborately prepared for, more explicitly rendered. Furthermore, the novel not only records the spiritual corruption of De Soto; it also records the less dramatic but no less final corruption of Tovar, the center of consciousness through most of the action, whose besetting sins are of the flesh rather than the spirit. In another letter concerning the novel, Mr. Lytle wrote of De Soto and Tovar that,

> They find no gold, but in their search for it the two men ... each the obverse of the other, accept the world and become protestant or unchristian. De Soto by will, Tovar by the senses, the two men who always accept the world.... In their persons is the symbol of the overthrow of Christendom.[3]

Accepting the world by will is not the same, except in the final result, as accepting it by the senses. Both, of course, require rejection of God; but Tovar's sensibility is the perfect complement to De Soto's will. Together they provide an image of that rebellion of will and passion that is sin. De Soto is another Overreacher, the spiritual descendant of Prometheus, of Faustus (or more accurately perhaps of Tamburlaine), and of Lucifer. His sin, like that of his predecessors, is pride, the preference of one's own will to the will of God, the refusal to accept the limitations of fallen human nature, and the ultimate deification of self. Promethean pride is total subjectivity. Reality for De Soto is dependent on his perception of it; what he wills becomes reality. Throughout the novel, the Mass, the perfect enactment of the self-sacrifice of Christ and ideally of communicant, stands in contrast to De Soto's destructive subjectivity. The more the wilderness threatens his grand dream of conquest, the more monstrously obsessed he becomes until, at the novel's climax, with titanic presumption he rejects

---

2 "Toward a Dark Shape: Lytle's 'Alchemy' and the Conquest of the New World," *Mississippi Quarterly*, 23 (Fall 1970), 407–410. This essay is reprinted in this volume.

3 Polk, p. 456.

God, asserts the supremacy of his private vision, and shortly there-
after dies. It is only dead that the Adelantado understands that "the
will is not enough."

Tovar's acceptance of the world lacks the Promethean stature of
his leader's sin, but in this man of the senses Mr. Lytle has created an
ideal center of consciousness. Reflective by nature, Tovar comments
in some depth on De Soto's pride and will. And yet he is only partially
capable of seeing or resisting the danger of his captain's presumption.
Influenced both by De Soto's determination and by his own devotion
to the flesh, Tovar is a flawed narrator, and his account of the Spanish expedition is, therefore, dramatic. Tension and suspense are not
only inherent in his literal account of the army's wanderings, but also
in his attempts to understand and interpret the will that moves the
army and his own subjugation to that will.

Unlike De Soto, for whom will is reality, Tovar accepts the testi-
mony of his senses concerning the reality of the world; but he errs in
denying the goodness of creation. In attempting to avoid responsibility for his actions, he sees evil in nature and fails to see it in the human
heart. When he seduces Doña Ysabel's lady, Leonora, in the forest, he
regards the place as evil: "We alone, two Christians, are alone in this
place, wandering by ways known only to the things that crawl, and
that fly, and that creep. O Christ, the wild dogs." [4] Later he goes to
find a priest, presumably to confess, but upon finding greenery sprout-
ing from the rough-hewn Sanctuary, he cries out, "The sap, Father!
In God's house. ... The wilderness grows here too" (p.92). In Florida, as the army faces the wilderness, Tovar thinks, "At last the Governor had met his adversary" (p.277). Because Tovar can perceive
no reality outside of nature, he is obsessed with his own manhood
through which he attempts unsuccessfully to dominate the world.[5]
And because he regards nature as evil, he can never be too critical of
De Soto, the man who sets his will against both nature and God. Tovar
follows De Soto to the end, occasionally with reservations, but never
totally renouncing his part in the Governor's monomania.

Human self-assertion through passion and through will is embodied
in Tovar and De Soto, and their journey into the wilderness is a type

[4] *At the Moon's Inn* (Indianapolis: The Bobbs-Merrill Co., 1941), p. 89. All
subsequent references to the novel will be included in the text.
[5] The end of Tovar's sexuality is self-gratification, not procreation.

of the descent into hell. Each is finally defeated at his own level; the world always betrays those who follow it. Tovar's manhood is shown to be inferior to that of a savage, and De Soto's will is at the last capable only of self-destruction. The journey motif, used since Homer to show changing spiritual conditions as well as physical movement, serves well to record the futility of these fragmented views of reality and the inevitable defeat of the men who cling to them.

Before examining the expedition itself, however, I would like to look closely at the opening chapter of the novel, "The Feast." In his essay "Andrew Lytle," Thomas Carter criticizes this chapter for being "overlong." [6] But he fails to see the way in which the opening functions not only in establishing the characters of De Soto and Tovar and the nature of the Spanish undertaking, but also in clarifying a key assumption. What a man is precedes what he does. Had the novel dealt exclusively with De Soto's trek through the South, the reader might have been tempted, as Tovar was, to blame the wilderness for the deterioration of the explorer's soul, to find evil in nature instead of in man. "The Feast" prevents such a misreading. Before the expedition ever leaves Spain, we are convinced beyond question that it is a hellish voyage made by men consumed by pride and avarice.

The novel opens in San Lúcar with Tovar telling Silvestre, a young man eager to go to Florida, how he became involved in the Peruvian expedition. Having driven a herd of fighting bulls to Seville, the eighteen-year-old Tovar lost his innocence with a girl named María. She had him robbed, shamed him publicly, and finally involved him in a knife fight in which he killed his opponent. To escape the gallows, he fled to the New World. Thinking back to the day he drove the bulls into Seville, Tovar recalls his naiveté: "how little I knew that for myself, as well as for my charges, had begun the first slow steps in the long dance of death" (p.11).[7] From the outset, Tovar's deepest commit-

[6] In *South: Modern Southern Literature in Its Cultural Setting*, ed. Louis D. Rubin, Jr., and Robert D. Jacobs (Garden City: Doubleday and Co., 1961), p. 292.

[7] The bullfight plays no part in the novel, but Tovar's sympathy for the bulls is revealing. The bullfight is a ritual dramatization of the human confrontation with death, with the bestial element in human nature, with the world. It is a dance of death for which the appropriate end is the death of the bull, symbolic of the defeat of the world, of triumph over the incarnation of evil; and yet Tovar laments the defeat of the bulls: "and I thought must pride and passion come to this, be hung to the mild feet of the gelded" (p.11).

ment is to the world, and his flight to escape hanging is a paradigm of the whole New World venture, an attempt both intellectual and emotional to escape or deny the effects of the Fall.[8]

Near death in Panama, Tovar is rescued by De Soto. De Soto's voice calls the dying Tovar back from "that sweet weakness which despises the world" (p.19). In our first glimpse of De Soto, his eyes testify to his self-devouring pride:

> Sharp and lustrous, never eyes to be taken by surprise, and yet I had the feeling they rather looked in than out and looked not to see but to devour. . . . they seemed to be sinking into his flesh towards that dark interior where lay the only sustenance able to glut their hunger. (p.20)

Later in the first chapter, in a recollection by De Soto's wife, we learn that her husband as a boy, a page in her father's house, "stood apart, strong in pride even then" (p.21). And the boy was enthralled by Don Pedro's tales of his adventures in the Indies. He told of an abundance of gold and "of the times they chased the savages with Irish hounds for sport, and once how a certain captain hanged thirteen by the feet in the name of Our Lord and His twelve Apostles" (p.29). Only the Marquesa de Moya expresses horror at these atrocities and laments that "Christians would mock Holy Mary's Son in such a way" (p.29). The quest for gold and self-glorification makes beasts of men, and Don Pedro's chilling tale proves prophetic. In Florida De Soto too will make sport of throwing Indians to the dogs, will mock Holy Mary's Son and openly defy Him.

The central scene of the opening chapter is the dinner to which De Soto invites adventurers interested in joining his Florida expedition; some of the guests, like Tovar, are veterans of the Peruvian conquest; others, like Silvestre and young Hernandarias, are simply greedy, drawn to this dance of death by the desire for gold. Looking in briefly at her husband's guests, Doña Ysabel sees "a hateful ilumination on Hernan's face and in the eyes of his companions. . . . but neither in the Heavens nor in the earth did this light find its source. It set the guests' eyes ablaze, and yet it chilled. It glowed upon their faces; yet they were white and stricken" (pp.41–42). This chilling blaze, like the

---

[8] I am grateful for this suggestion to Professor M.E. Bradford.

flames in Milton's hell that shed "no light, but rather darkness visible," burns only in the hearts of the damned.

In the midst of this devilish gathering, however, there are two prophetic voices who try unsuccessfully to restore sanity, to prevent the expedition. The first of these voices belongs to an old Marshal of Seville, whom Bradford describes as "a crusader and true knight who serves well as a mouthpiece for the Godsweal of medieval Spain" (p.60, this volume). The Marshal is an old warrior who knows well the glory of battle "When the quarrel is just" (p.46), and he has already tried to dissuade his grandson Hernandarias from joining De Soto, assuring him that "lances may be broke for the Holy Cross in Africa, where the infidels still plot and dream of field and tower we drove them from" (p.45). But he also knows that the search for gold is not undertaken in the service of the Cross. To a priest who advances that argument the Marshal responds,

> I know . . . what is brought from those islands and continents which block the route to Cathay. And I ask you, priest, are we merchants and Jews? Shall we let perish our immortal souls for a policy like unto that of the Venetian state which pays tribute to Soliman that courtesans may have spices in their meats, that prelates may swell their tongues with saffron? (p.46)

Condemning Columbus for making "such a hole in Christendom I fear me it can never be plugged," the old Marshal thunders a toast: "Señores, I give you poverty, that poverty of the Cross which is Spain" (p.47). But he drinks alone.

This warning from the lips of one unfamiliar with the lands beyond the sea is complemented by the warning of Cabeza de Vaca, one of the survivors of the De Narváez expedition to Florida. As De Vaca enters the hall where De Soto and the others are assembled, a page tells Doña Ysabel, "It is Saint Lazarus come from the dead" (p.42). De Vaca tells a tale of starvation and cannibalism among the Spaniards. The adventurers are hungry for reports of gold, but he tells them that the greatest treasure in Florida is maize; he shows them a lacet "all that is left of the skin of His Majesty's factor," and a buskin which "once covered the back of a captain of foot"(p.58). After the dinner, when De Soto tells his wife of De Vaca's "trick," she realizes that in this horrid revelation "the Enemy had made himself tangible," and she speaks of Florida as a land "abandoned of God, the very principality of the world, where renunciation must forever fail" (pp.61–62). Cannibalism becomes an emblem of total acceptance of the world: "There could be no more abandoned acceptance of the world than for brother to eat his brother! Eat of the everdying flesh and go down quick into hell" (p.62). She pleads with De Soto to give up his vision of conquest; but her pleading is vain, and in the closing scene of "The Feast," as he makes love to her against her will, she realizes the extent of her husband's presumption: "Her head whirled as thick and stifling pressed down upon her a sweet and unbearable odour. It was that of corrupting flesh! Cannibal" (p.68). Sex is for De Soto simply another way of asserting his will, and the description of his assault suggests intercourse with an incubus: "And then like a thing out of the night she heard his voice, harsh through stops of breath, and the deep bare chest hovering above her, the long shadow descending" (p.67).

The account of De Soto's wanderings, which begins in Chapter Three, "The Wilderness," and occupies the rest of the novel, is a masterpiece of narrative compression and selection. Without ignoring the geographic or chronological scope of his material, Mr. Lytle includes nothing that does not contribute to his theme. Every scene provides evidence of the damnable futility of the expedition; each chapter shows the increasing discontent of the army, the increasing monomania of its leader.[9] Based on his experience in Peru, De Soto has preconceived notions about the Indians in Florida and what it will take to subdue them. As he puts it, "The devil is cunning . . . but I understand his policy. . . . All power lies in the person of the Indian ruler. Seize him and his subjects will obey us" (p.117). However true this observation may have been of the Peruvian Indians, it was certainly not true of the tribes of North America; but in spite of bitter experience to the contrary, the man of will never changes his tactics, cannot accept anything as true which contradicts his will. Ironically his statement that "all power lies in the person of the Indian ruler" is increasingly true of his own command as discontent grows among the

[9] For a full discussion of Mr. Lytle's use of the historical accounts of De Soto's expedition, see Chapter Three, "Alchemy in Men," in Charles C. Clark's "The Novels of Andrew Lytle: A Study in the Artistry of Fiction" (Unpublished Ph.D. dissertation, Louisiana State University, May 1972).

Spaniards. And in a variety of ways the Indians continue to resist, to defy and harass the invaders despite the capture of several tribal chiefs.

As I mentioned earlier, the offering of self which the Mass both enacts and requires contrasts throughout the novel to De Soto's pride. The Mass also functions in the account of the journey as a structural device. Three particularly notable Masses are celebrated in Florida: each one is either the occasion of an important action or serves as a prologue to a significant scene or action. Each one is followed by a specific act of brutality by the Christians, an explicit contradiction of all that the Mass is and represents. De Soto orders a woman thrown to the dogs after the first Mass, burns an Indian at the stake after the second, and orders a massacre after the third. Each atrocity is less justifiable in terms of policy than the one before it, pointing unmistakably to the growing corruption of the Governor's soul.

The occasion of the first Mass, celebrated in "The Wilderness," is the recovery of Juan Ortiz, also a survivor of De Narváez's party, who has lived as an Indian captive for twelve years and who serves De Soto as interpreter after his rescue. Ortiz's captivity is relived in his consciousness during the celebration of a Mass.[10] This stream of consciousness recollection is handled with great skill; portions of the liturgy trigger Ortiz's memory of significant segments of his life among the savages. For example, at the *Kyrie*, the liturgical cry for God's blessing, Ortiz remembers: "Mercy, mercy, mercy. He was lying on the floor of a cabin, his dry lips moving in supplication"(p.129). He has been rescued from burning by Indian women. At the Offertory, as Fr. Francisco offers "this unspotted Host," Ortiz recalls the nights he was made to guard the Indian burial ground, a place filled with ghosts "crying blood for blood that they may travel west. . . . to the land of the Breath Holder"(p.137). Through Ortiz's recollection we learn much about the Indians. And perhaps the most important thing, the thing which separates the Indians from the Spaniards, is that their lives are controlled by their religious convictions and rituals. These Indians are not pre-lapsarian noble savages, but they recognize

---

[10] "Ortiz's Mass" has been published separately in *A Novel, a Novella, and Four Stories* (New York: McDowell, Obolensky, Inc., 1958), pp. 67–100.

in ritual a way of ordering their lives, of living intimately with nature without being overwhelmed. In his essay "Caroline Gordon and the Historic Image," Mr. Lytle says of the Indians,

> A religious people, their behavior was governed by fear of and identity with the power of nature. The supernatural existed as an extension of nature. . . . In their positive identity with the natural world, families traced their descent from the beast, the fish, or even the wind. The preservation and continuance of life, therefore, became the center of their religious practice, the dignity of man and the rites of hospitality its corollaries. Their warfare did not evince a destructive instinct. It was a religious rite, and therefore a social rite, which submerged the end of fighting which is death beneath the ritual practice of it.[11]

The deepest convictions of Christendom are expressed in the ritual of the Mass, and yet De Soto's army in no way lives that ritual. Ortiz received mercy at the hands of savages, but immediately after Ortiz's Mass, the Christians who had cried *Kyrie, eleison* show a singular lack of mercy in their treatment of an Indian captive.

Ortiz himself not only serves the practical function of interpreter; he also sees, albeit dimly, the wickedness of the Spanish venture. As an outsider, a man in many ways more Indian than Spanish, he does not have the stake in the conquest that Tovar does; and after the army occupies and transforms the village in which he was a captive, Ortiz notes that "It would have taken the Indians years, with fires at the trunks of the trees, to have cleared away such a space. De Soto had done it in a week. That was a dangerous, hostile act, an act of magic" (p.158).

The march inland is difficult. Food is scarce; the Indians are hostile, the swampland treacherous, and at every village hope of finding gold fades. As morale declines, some of the men talk of turning back, but De Soto is adamant, and through his determination and physical courage he succeeds in establishing the supremacy of his will: "he had exposed his person to a greater risk than any other under his command. Now his will was the army's will. No longer would he need to force it. He was free for his task"(p.255). In the context of this almost

---

[11] *The Hero with the Private Parts* (Baton Rouge: Louisiana State University Press, 1966), p. 157.

hopeless determination, the second Mass in Florida is celebrated. Lost in the woods of what is now Georgia, the army attends Mass especially to pray for deliverance. As Fr. Francisco starts to elevate the chalice, he finds "a poisonous worm crawling up the side of the cup . . . sloth-fully drawing its back and swinging its head over the Sacred Blood" (p.287). Fr. Francisco prays that the thing will die, and "suddenly the worm shrivelled and fell to the ground." God has prevented mind-less nature from defiling the Sacrament, and the army rejoices, De Soto leading in the singing of the *Te Deum*. Yet within a few days the Governor burns an Indian at the stake for refusing to talk.

This second Mass serves as a prologue to the army's stay at Cuti-fichiqui, a significant station in its descent into the New World's heart of darkness. Here a confrontation occurs between De Soto and Fr. Francisco which prefigures De Soto's final rejection of God, and here Tovar perceives the destructive nature of De Soto's idea of conquest. "[De Soto] delayed, neither conquering nor moving on but ravaging the land, taking away the liberty of the Indians without converting them"(p.306). Tovar himself regards Cutifichiqui as an "earthly para-dise," [12] and longs to remain there in idyllic bliss, to stop wandering. He even briefly imagines that with the discovery of pearls De Soto might be willing to settle. But in fact he knows that for the Governor Cutifichiqui is only a temporary stop; and in the disappointment of the high hopes he had held for the place, in a kind of childish rebellion, Tovar marries the Indian woman, Tsianina. This marriage, however, marks no real break between Tovar and De Soto. As Tovar realizes, "He had followed De Soto out of Cuba to aid, not do him hurt. Cer-tainly it was a gratuitous hurt, and foolish, and unjust to hold the Governor to account for all that he, Tovar, had hoped for from Cutifichiqui" (p.320–321). He cannot bring himself to defy De Soto's demonic will. The man of the senses cannot resist the man of will, for both have accepted the world.

Greeted courteously by the woman who rules Cutifichiqui, the Spaniards attend the festival of the mulberry moon. Fr. Francisco declares that "It is a feast of death"(p.299) and forbids Christian participation. De Soto defies him. Attending the moon festival is symbolic of the Spaniards' "acceptance of the world," and the mean-

[12] Polk, p. 456.

ing of the novel's title becomes clear. As the priest points out, the moon is the "pagan goddess of the woods and fields and streams," and "at the moon's inn" which "is a Spanish phrase . . . meaning literally to sleep out in the open," [13] comes in the course of the novel to mean life in the world. In Chapter One, young Tovar in a crowded kitchen in Seville had thought to himself how much easier it would be for him to breathe "at the moon's inn" (p.12). At Cutifichiqui De Soto accuses Tovar of being moon-struck for marrying the Indian woman; Tovar replies, "Mayhap we are all moon-struck"(p.325). And finally, at the end of the novel De Soto's ghost tells Tovar, "There is no remedy. For you or me, or any who come to this land. It is the Moon's Inn for all, heathen and Christian alike. It can never be more than a temporary abode, a stopping place of the variable seasons, where the moon is host and the reckoning counted up in sweat, in hunger, and in blood" (p.397). So is life in the world, and that hard lesson De Soto learns too late. As Tovar realizes at Cutifichiqui, "Following De Soto, the Christians had stumbled upon the world and before any knew it, all were drawn fast by its coils" (p.324).

Before the third Mass which is the novel's climax, the army fights a nearly disastrous battle with the Indians at Mauvilla (in South Alabama). In addition to preparing for the climax, this battle reveals the perversity of Tovar's spirit, the depth of his involvement in the world. The battle is so fierce that the Spaniards' only hope of victory lies in burning the village, and the final combats are fought in the midst of an inferno. Tovar is at last aware "that behind the painted masks and streaming feathers there were men fighting for their lives" (p.355); and yet as he pursues a single Indian with his lance, which an arrow has pierced to form a cross, we see that a man of the senses seeks in flesh a self-deification:

> Freed from the confusion and the frenzy of the melee, the threat of arrows hissing from unknown and unseen directions, alone with his enemy, surrounded by fire, alone and triumphant . . . so did Tovar prolong his sense of power, godlike in its aloofness, all danger to his person remote, playing with his enemy as upon a hunt, pricking him never deeper than half an inch to increase his fury, delaying the inevitable stroke of death. (pp.355–356)

[13] *Ibid.*

Tovar's triumph is thwarted as the Indian leaps into a burning house to avoid death at his enemy's hand. The savage stands in the flames looking out on "the enemy he had humbled by his superior act of manhood"(p.356).

Spanish losses at Mauvilla are heavy: twenty-two are dead, 250 wounded, and most of their supplies are destroyed, including their hoard of pearls from Cutifichiqui and the communion vessels. Tovar notes that the loss of the pearls makes De Soto "gloomy and withdrawn"(p.360). The Governor's will, his belief in the conquest, remains firm, however; and his self-confidence is apparent in his rejection of the Church's authority, his rejection of God. In the climactic scene, celebrating Mass with the last wafer rescued from Mauvilla, Fr. Francisco stops before making his communion, calls De Soto before him, and by the authority of the Sacrament orders him to "Go out of this land"(p.368). The priest trespasses in a matter of policy and is himself corrupted by "all the arrogance of spiritual pride"(p.369); and yet once Fr. Francisco has thus used his office and the Body of Christ, De Soto cannot, except at the risk of his soul, disobey. The Governor's response is blunt: "I believe it is God's will that this land be pacified. Pacified it shall be" (p.373). The logical extension of pride is now complete:

> He had set his private will outside the guidance and discipline of the Church, the will which, unrestrained, serves only the senses, as the senses only the flesh. He, a layman, had undertaken to interpret God's mind. This is what his decision meant, no matter if he denied or disguised it. From here it is only one step further to supplant God's will by man's and call it divine—man made God, man with all his frailties and pride setting up the goods of this world over the good of heavenly grace. (p.374) [14]

De Soto's action repeats that preference for private judgment demonstrated by Lucifer, by Adam, and all his children since Eden; that the exploitation of the New World was a reenactment of that original disobedience is the point of *At the Moon's Inn*. Tovar's summary

---

[14] In his essay on Caroline Gordon, Mr. Lytle says, "Each long hunter, each frontiersman became a primitive, homespun Dr. Faustus. Having dismissed the Devil along with God (the Protestant belief in a private communion with God is equivalent to Man-become-God), man no longer had any defense against his violation of the laws of nature, nor any absolute set of principles to which he might refer the processes of reason" (*Hero*, p. 158).

indicates that he knows precisely to what spiritual depths the army has sunk, and yet "he turned his back upon the altar. He turned and faced the wilderness" (p.374). He assents to De Soto's blasphemy and in assenting takes the burden of that sin upon himself.

The novel is quickly and skillfully ended after the climax. The final chapter, "The Conquest," is set in an encampment on the Mississippi River two years after Mauvilla. De Soto is dying of fever, but his will remains unshaken. Tovar thinks "he might even stumble upon the golden city"(p.385). But completely isolated, the will is now totally corrupt, both in De Soto and his army; and when the Governor sends Tovar with a small force to terrorize the Nilco, women and children are slaughtered. Tovar "had seen a baby thrown into the air as a target" (p.390). Hurrying back to camp to assure De Soto that his will has been done, Tovar's conscience is troubled; but he can still perceive no higher end than pleasing the Governor, restoring his health.

De Soto dies before Tovar returns, however, and what he encounters is the Governor's ghost. Thinking he is addressing a living man, he tries to be cheerful: "I did not fail you. Do not despair. All may yet go well. The will remains"(p.397). But it is too late, and dead De Soto announces at last what he refused to learn while alive:

> The will is not enough. It is not enough for one bent on his own destruction. Did I lead the chivalry of Spain to the sacred groves, the blessed land of Jerusalem? No, I am the alchemical captain, the adventurer in gold. Gold the wanderer. (p.397)

At the Moon's Inn is a significant work of historical fiction and should be reprinted. The development of the theme is sure, and the trek itself is vividly rendered; the battle at Mauvilla is as skillfully written as any fictional battle I know. In spite of the burden of repeated confrontations with different groups of Indians, Mr. Lytle maintains tension and suspense at every stage of the journey. That *At the Moon's Inn* has not received wider critical notice is more an indictment of modern critical judgment (or, indeed, of modern society) than it is of the novel. To read the novel rightly, one must first accept the significance of De Soto's defiance of Fr. Francisco and the Host, the reality of the alternatives open to him: God or Satan. The reader who refuses to accept this reality loses much more than the appreciation of a fine novel.

An Andrew Lytle Checklist

NOEL POLK

I. PRIMARY

A. Separate Publications

1931 *Bedford Forrest and His Critter Company* (biography). New York: Minton, Balch & Company. [i]–ix, [1]–390, [391]–402 pp.

New York: G.P. Putnam's Sons, [1935]. [i]–ix, [1]–390, [391]–402 pp.

London: Eyre & Spottiswoode, 1938. [i]–ix, [1]–390, [391]–402 pp.

London: Eyre & Spottiswoode, 1939. With a foreword by B.H. Liddell Hart. [i]–xi, [1]–390, [391]–402 pp.

New York: McDowell, Obolensky, [1960?]. With an introduction by the Author. [i]–xvii, [1]–390, [391]–402, 403 pp.

1936 *The Long Night* (novel). Indianapolis, New York: The Bobbs-Merrill Company. [1–9], [11]–331 pp.

New York: Grossett & Dunlap, 1938. [Information from trade lists. I have not seen a copy.]

London: Eyre & Spottiswoode, 1937. [Information from publisher's files. I have not seen a copy.]

1941 *At the Moon's Inn* (novel). Indianapolis, New York: The Bobbs-Merrill Company. [i], [1–5], [7]–400 pp.

London: Eyre & Spottiswoode, 1943. [1–5], 7–333 pp.

Värdshuset Månen: Berättelsen om Hernando de Sotos expedition till Florida. Translated into Swedish by Nils Holmberg. Stockholm: Förlagsaktiebolaget A. Sohlman & Co., 1943.

1947 *A Name for Evil* (novel). Indianapolis, New York: The Bobbs-Merrill Company. [1–7], 9–215 pp.

New York: Avon Books, 1969. (Wrappers.)

97

1957 *The Velvet Horn* (novel). New York: McDowell, Obolensky. [i–v], [1]–373, [375] pp.

1958 *A Novel, A Novella and Four Stories.* New York: Mc Dowell, Obolensky. With a foreword by the author. [i–xx], [1]–327, [329] pp.
      Contains: FOREWORD——JERICHO, JERICHO, JERICHO——THE MA-HOGANY FRAME——MR. MACGREGOR——ORTIZ'S MASS——ALCHEMY ——A NAME FOR EVIL.

1964 *A Christian University and the Word: An Address for Found-ers' Day [October 10,] 1964.* (Speech given at the University of the South, Sewanee, Tennessee). [1–8] pp. Printed wrap-pers. Distributed by the Development Office of the University of the South. Re-issued [n.d.] in a slightly altered format, with-out the sub-title. [1–8] pp.

1966 *The Hero With the Private Parts* (essays). Baton Rouge: Lou-isiana State University Press. With a foreword by Allen Tate and a preface by the Author. [i]–xx, [1]–239 pp.
      Contains: FOREWORD——PREFACE——THE IMAGE AS GUIDE TO MEAN-ING IN THE HISTORICAL NOVEL——IN DEFENSE OF A PASSIONATE AND INCORRUPTIBLE HEART——THE HERO WITH THE PRIVATE PARTS—— THE OPEN BOAT: A PAGAN TALE——THE DISPLACED FAMILY——A MOVE-ABLE FEAST: THE GOING TO AND FRO——THE SON OF MAN: HE WILL PREVAIL——REGENERATION FOR THE MAN——THE TOWN: HELEN'S LAST STAND——CAROLINE GORDON AND THE HISTORIC IMAGE——NOTE ON A TRADITIONAL SENSIBILITY——ALLEN TATE: UPON THE OCCASION OF HIS SIXTIETH BIRTHDAY——THE WORKING NOVELIST AND THE MYTHMAKING PROCESS——FOREWORD TO A NOVEL, A NOVELLA, AND FOUR STORIES——JOHN C. CALHOUN——R.E. LEE.

1971 *Craft and Vision: The Best Fiction from "The Sewanee Re-view,"* edited and with a foreword by Andrew Lytle. New York: Delacorte Press.

B. Periodical Contributions
Introductions

1. Stories

"Old Scratch in the Valley." *Virginia Quarterly Review,* 8 (April 1932), 237–246.

"Mister McGregor." *Virginia Quarterly Review,* 11 (January-Octo-ber 1935), 218–227. Reprinted in *NN4S.*

"Jericho, Jericho, Jericho." *Southern Review,* 1 (Spring 1936), 753–764. Reprinted in *NN4S.*

"A Fragment: How Nuno de Tovar Came To Cross The Ocean Sea."

Hika (student literary magazine of Kenyon College), 5 (June 1939), 5–8. A fragment of a "work in progress," from *At the Moon's Inn.*

"Alchemy." *Kenyon Review*, 4 (Autumn 1942), 273–327. Mr. Lytle conceived and wrote this story as a prologue for *At the Moon's Inn*, and then decided against using it as such.[1] Reprinted in *NN4S.*

"The Guide." *Sewanee Review*, 53 (July 1945), 362–387. Reprinted in *NN4S* under the title "The Mahogany Frame."

"The Mahogany Frame." See "The Guide."

"What Quarter of the Night." *Sewanee Review*, 64 (Summer 1956), 349–397. Corresponds roughly to "The Water Witch" section of *The Velvet Horn.*

"Ortiz's Mass" was first published as pp. 122–150 of *At the Moon's Inn*, then reprinted as one of the stories in *NN4S.*

2. Memoirs

"A Wake for the Living." *Sewanee Review*, 75 (Autumn 1967), 585–627.

"The Garden of Innocence." *Sewanee Review*, 79 (January-March 1971), 70–85.

"The Old Neighborhood." *Southern Review*, 8 n.s. (October 1972), 816–835.

3. Poetry

"Hill Cattle." In *Driftwood Flames.* Nashville: The Poetry Guild, [1923], p. 22.

"*Une Reflexion.*" In *Driftwood Flames*, p. 45.

"Edward Graves." *The Fugitive*, 4 (March 1925), 17.

4. Essays/Reviews

"Andrew Lytle, Le Grand Homme." *Little Tiger*, 4 (Christmas 1920), 5. The *Little Tiger* was a publication of the students of Sewanee Military Academy, Sewanee, Tennessee, from which Mr. Lytle graduated in 1920. This is a letter—as far as I am able to tell, the author's earliest publication—from Mr. Lytle, from abroad, to a Major Gass of the Academy. The return address is given as: 132 Rue Paissy, St. Germain-En-Lage, France. The title under which it is recorded here is a headline, not Mr. Lytle's title.

"The Hind Tit." In *I'll Take My Stand: The South and the Agrarian Tradition* by "Twelve Southerners." New York: Harper & Brothers, 1930, pp. 201–245.

[1] Interview, January 1970, Monteagle, Tennessee.

"Life in the Cotton Belt." *New Republic*, 67 (3 June 1931), 77–78. Review of *The Forge* by T. S. Stribling.

"Lytle, Huntsville Author, Advocates Forrest Statue." Interview with Mr. Lytle. Huntsville, Alabama, *Times*, 22 July 1931, p. 4.

"The Lincoln Myth." *Virginia Quarterly Review*, 7 (October 1931), 620–626. Review of *Lincoln, The Man* by Edgar Lee Masters, *Lincoln the Politician* by Don C. Seitz, *New Letters and Papers of Lincoln* by Paul M. Angle, and *Europe and the American Civil War* by Donaldson Jordan and Edward Pratt.

"Principles of Secession," *Hound and Horn*, 5 (July–September 1932), 687–693. Review of *Robert Barnwell Rhett, Father of Secession* by Laura White, and *Edmund Ruffin, Southerner* by Avery Craven.

"A Tactical Blunder." *Virginia Quarterly Review*, 9 (April 1933), 300–303. Review of *Sherman: Fighting Prophet* by Lloyd Lewis.

"The Backwoods Progression." *American Review*, 1 (September 1933), 409–434.

"John Taylor and the Political Economy of Agriculture." *American Review*, 3 (September 1934), 432–447; 3 (October 1934), 630–643; 4 (November 1934), 84–99.

"The Passion of Alex Maury." *New Republic*, 81 (2 January, 1935), 227–228. Review of *Aleck Maury, Sportsman* by Caroline Gordon.

"Follow the Furies." *Southern Review*, 1 (July 1935), 203–205. Review of *Follow the Furies* by Eleanor Carroll Chilton.

"R. E. Lee." *Southern Review*, 1 (July 1935), 411–422. Review of *R. E. Lee* by D. S. Freeman. Reprinted in *Hero*.

"The Approach of the Southern Writer to His Material." *The Atlanta Constitution* (Book Section), 29 November 1936, p. 14.

"The Small Farm Secures the State." In *Who Owns America?*, edited by Herbert Agar and Allen Tate. Boston: Houghton Mifflin, 1936, pp. 237–250.

"John C. Calhoun." *Southern Review*, 3 (Winter 1938), 510–530. Review of *The Cast Iron Man, John C. Calhoun and American Democracy* by Arthur Styron. Reprinted in *Hero*.

"Lee's Lieutenants." *Sewanee Review*, 51 (Winter 1943), 177–179. Review of *Lee's Lieutenants* by D. S. Freeman.

"At Heaven's Gate." *Sewanee Review*, 51 (Autumn 1943), 599–602. Review of *At Heaven's Gate* by Robert Penn Warren.

"Note on a Traditional Sensibility." *Sewanee Review*, 56 (Summer 1948), 370–373. Tribute to John Crowe Ransom. Reprinted in *Hero*.

"Regeneration for the Man." *Sewanee Review*, 57 (Winter 1949), 120–127. Essay-review of *Intruder in the Dust* by William Faulkner. Reprinted in *Hero*.

"Caroline Gordon and the Historic Image." *Sewanee Review*, 57 (Autumn 1949), 560–586. Reprinted in *Hero*.

"The Agrarians Today: A Symposium." *Shenandoah*, 3 (Summer 1952), 14–33. Mr. Lytle contributed pp. 30–32.

"How Many Miles to Babylon?" *Hopkins Review*, 6 (Spring–Summer 1953), 101–104. Reprinted on pp. 31–34 of *Southern Renascence: The Literature of the Modern South*, ed. Louis D. Rubin, Jr., and Robert D. Jacobs. Baltimore: The Johns Hopkins Press, 1953.

"The Image as Guide to Meaning in the Historical Novel." *Sewanee Review*, 61 (Summer 1953), 408–426. Reprinted in *Hero*.

"The Old Country Store." *Southern Folklore Quarterly*, 18 (December 1954), 246–247. Review of *The Old Country Store* by Gerald Carson.

"The Son of Man: He Will Prevail." *Sewanee Review*, 63 (Winter 1955), 114–137. Essay-review of *A Fable* by William Faulkner. Reprinted in *Hero*.

"A Summing Up." *Shenandoah*, 6 (Summer 1955), 28–36.

"The Forest of the South." *Critique*, 1 (Winter 1956), 3–9. Discussion of *The Forest of the South* by Caroline Gordon.

"A Hero and the Doctrinaires of Defeat." *Georgia Review*, 10 (Winter 1956), 453–467.

"*The Town*: Helen's Last Stand." *Sewanee Review*, 65 (Summer 1957), 475–484. Essay-review of *The Town* by William Faulkner. Reprinted in *Hero*.

"The Quality of the South." *National Review*, 5 (8 March 1958), 236–237. Review of *The Lasting South*, ed. James Kilpatrick and Louis Rubin, Jr.

"The Working Novelist and the Mythmaking Process." *Daedalus*, 88 (Spring 1959), 326–338. Reprinted in *Hero*.

"Foreword," *A Novel, a Novella and Four Stories*. New York: McDowell, Obolensky, 1958. Reprinted in *Hero*.

"Introduction" to the McDowell, Obolensky issue of *Bedford Forrest* (New York, 1958), pp. xi–xvii.

"Man or Symbol?" *National Review*, 6 (6 December 1958), 375. Review of Brainard Cheney's *This Is Adam* and Richard Wright's *The Long Dream*.

"The Displaced Family." *Sewanee Review*, 66 (Winter 1958), 115–131. Essay-review of *Sojourn of a Stranger* by Walter Sullivan, *The Homecoming Game* by Howard Nemerov, and *Tennessee Day in St. Louis* by Peter Taylor. Reprinted in *Hero*.

Fugitives' Reunion: Conversations at Vanderbilt May 3–5, 1956. Edited by Rob Roy Purdy. Nashville: Vanderbilt University Press, [1959]. Mr. Lytle contributed often to the discussions.

"Allen Tate: Upon the Occasion of his Sixtieth Birthday." *Sewanee Review*, 67 (October–December 1959), 542–544. Reprinted in *Hero*.

"Agee's Letters to Father Flye." *Sewanee Review*, 71 (Winter 1963), 164–165. Review of *Letters of James Agee to Father Flye*.

"Impressionism, The Ego, and The First Person." *Daedalus*, 92 (Spring 1963), 281–296. Reprinted in *Hero* under the title "The Hero with the Private Parts."

"*A Moveable Feast*: The Going To and Fro." *Sewanee Review*, 73 (Spring 1965), 339–343. Review of Hemingway's posthumous book. Reprinted in *Hero*.

"In Defense of a Passionate and Incorruptible Heart." *Sewanee Review*, 73 (Autumn 1965), 593–615. An examination of *Madame Bovary*. Reprinted in *Hero*.

" 'The Open Boat': A Pagan Tale," is first printed in *The Hero with the Private Parts*.

"The Hero With the Private Parts." See "Impressionism, The Ego, and The First Person."

"A Reading of Joyce's 'The Dead'." *Sewanee Review*, 77 (Spring 1969), 193–216.

"Foreword" to *The South: Old and New Frontiers; Selected Essays of Frank Lawrence Owsley*, ed. Harriet Chappell Owsley. Athens: University of Georgia Press, 1969, pp. ix–xiv.

"Foreword" to *Craft and Vision: The Best Fiction from "The Sewanee Review,"* ed. Andrew Lytle. New York: Delacorte Press, 1971, pp. vii–xi.

"The State of Letters in a Time of Disorder." *Sewanee Review*, 79 (Autumn 1971), 477–497.

II. SECONDARY

In the following checklist, I have tried to include all full-length essays dealing with Mr. Lytle's works, and a representative sampling of newspaper and periodical reviews, especially those which appear in the major literary review organs, or which are written by prominent literary figures. I have also included a selective list of items in which Mr. Lytle's work is mentioned and analyzed briefly, or is discussed in the context of another writer or group of writers or literary movement.

Amacher, A. W. "Myths and Consequences: Calhoun and Some Nashville Agrarians." *South Atlantic Quarterly*, 59 (Spring 1960), 251–264.

Anonymous. Review of *The Hero with the Private Parts*. *Virginia Quarterly Review*, 43 (Winter 1967), xxii.

————. "The Cropleigh Saga." *Time*, 70 (26 August 1957), 88. Reviews *The Velvet Horn*.

————. Review of *At the Moon's Inn*. *New Yorker*, 17 (22 November 1941), 94.

Barry, Iris. "A Selection of the Season's New Fiction." *Books*, 10 August 1947, 6. Reviews *A Name for Evil*.

Basso, Hamilton. "Orestes in Alabama." *New Republic*, 88 (30 September 1936), 231. Reviews *The Long Night*.

Benson, Carl. "Comments." In *The Deep South in Transformation*, ed. Robert Highsaw. University, Alabama: University of Alabama Press, 1964, pp. 161–166. Brief comments on *The Velvet Horn*, pp. 163–164.

Benson, Robert G. "The Progress of Hernando de Soto in Andrew Lytle's *At the Moon's Inn*." *Georgia Review*, 27 (Summer 1973), 232–244. Reprinted, revised somewhat, this collection as "Yankees of the Race: The Decline and Fall of Hernando de Soto."

Bowen, R. O. "Sons of the Soil." *Saturday Review*, 40 (17 August 1957), 13–14. Reviews *The Velvet Horn*.

Bradbury, John M. *The Fugitives: A Critical Account*. Chapel Hill: University of North Carolina Press, 1958. See index for numerous references to Lytle.

————. *Renaissance in the South: A Critical History of the Literature, 1920–1960*. Chapel Hill: University of North Carolina Press, 1963. See index for references to Lytle.

Bradford, M. E. "The Fiction of Andrew Lytle." *Mississippi Quarterly*, 23 (Fall 1970), 347–348.

————. "Toward a Dark Shape: Lytle's 'Alchemy' and the Conquest of the New World." *Mississippi Quarterly*, 23 (Fall 1970), 407–414. Reprinted this collection.

————. "A Gathering of Friends." *Religion and Society*, 2 (June 1969), 35–39. Pp. 37–39 review *Hero*.

————. "Andrew Lytle." In James Vinson, ed., *Contemporary Novelists*. New York: St. Martins, London: St. James Press, 1972, pp. 792–794.

————. "That Other Eden in the West: A Preface to Andrew Lytle." This collection.

Brooks, Cleanth. "The Old Order: *The Unvanquished* as an Account of the Disintegration of Society." In his *William Faulkner: The Yoknapatawpha Country*. New Haven: Yale University Press, 1963, pp. 93, 382–383. A brief discussion of Lytle's essay-review "The Son of Man: He will Prevail."

Brown, Ashley. "Andrew Nelson Lytle." In *A Bibliographical Guide to the Study of Southern Literature*, ed. Louis D. Rubin, Jr. Baton Rouge: LSU Press, 1969, p. 243.

Carter, Thomas H. "Andrew Lytle." In *South: Modern Southern Literature in its Cultural Setting*, ed., Louis D. Rubin, Jr., and Robert D. Jacobs. Garden City: Doubleday, 1961, pp. 287–300.

Clark, Charles C. "*A Name for Evil*: A Search for Order." *Mississippi Quarterly*, 23 (Fall 1970), 371–382. Reprinted this collection.

————. "The Novels of Andrew Lytle: A Study in the Artistry of Fiction." Unpublished doctoral dissertation, Louisiana State University, 1972.

Core, George. "A Mirror for Fiction: The Criticism of Andrew Lytle." *Georgia Review*, 22 (Summer 1968), 208–221. Essay-review of *The Hero with the Private Parts*.

Couch, W. T. "The Agrarian Romance." *South Atlantic Quarterly*, 36 (October 1937), 419–430. Pertinent to Lytle are pp. 427–428.

Cowan, Louise. *The Southern Critics*. Irving, Texas: University of Dallas Press, 1971, pp. 71–73.

Craven, Avery. Review of *Bedford Forrest*. *Books*, 28 June 1931, p. 7.

Davidson, Donald. "*I'll Take My Stand*: A History." *American Review*, 5 (Summer 1935), 301–321. Pertinent to Lytle are pp. 307, 312, 315.

Davis, Elmer. "A Striking First Novel." *Saturday Review of Literature*, 14 (12 September 1936), 11. Reviews *The Long Night*.

De Bellis, Jack. "The Southern Universe and the Counter-Renascence." *Southern Review*, 4 n.s. (Spring 1968), 471–481.

————. "An Andrew Nelson Lytle Checklist." Secretary's News Sheet, Bibliographical Society of the University of Virginia, No. 46. June, 1960.

————. "Andrew Lytle's *A Name for Evil*: A Transformation of *The Turn of the Screw*." *Critique*, 8 (Spring 1966), 26–40.

De Voto, Bernard. "Fiction Fights the Civil War." *Saturday Review of Literature*, 17 (18 December 1937), 1–2, 15–16. Pertinent to Lytle is p. 15.

Durham, Frank. "The Southern Literary Tradition: Shadow or Substance?" *South Atlantic Quarterly*, 67 (Summer 1968), 455–468.

Eisinger, Chester. *Fiction of the Forties*. Chicago: University of Chicago Press, 1963. Pp. 193–196 include discussions of *At the Moon's Inn* and *A Name for Evil*.

Fain, John Tyree. "Segments of Southern Renaissance." *South Atlantic Bulletin*. 36 (May 1971), 23–31. Pertinent to Lytle are pp. 23–27.

Farrelly, John. "Ghost Story." *New Republic*, 117 (25 August 1947), 31. Reviews *A Name for Evil*.

Field, L. M. "Conquerors in Florida." *New York Times Book Review*, 23 November 1941, p. 7. Review of *At the Moon's Inn*.

Geismar, Maxwell. "Mostly About the South." *Saturday Review*, 41 (30 August 1958), 12. Review of *A Novel, A Novella and Four Stories*.

Ghiselin, Brewster. "Trial of Light." *Sewanee Review*, 65 (Autumn 1957), 657–665. Reviews *The Velvet Horn*.

————. "Andrew Lytle's Selva Oscura." This collection.

Hart, B. H. Liddell. "Foreword" to London, 1939, issue of *Bedford Forrest*, pp. vii–viii.

Hendry, Irene. "Fiction Chronicle." *Sewanee Review*, 55 (Autumn 1947), 700–707. Pp. 706–707 concern *A Name for Evil*.

Hesseltine, W. B. "Look Away, Dixie." *Sewanee Review*, 39 (January–March 1931), 97–103. Reviews *I'll Take My Stand*. Pp. 100–101 are pertinent to Lytle.

Hoffman, Frederick J. *The Art of Southern Fiction: A Study of Some Modern Novelists*. Carbondale and Edwardsville, Illinois: Southern Illinois University Press, 1967. Pp. 99–102 discuss *The Long Night* and *The Velvet Horn*.

Holland, Robert B. "The Agrarian Manifesto—A Generation Later." *Mississippi Quarterly*, 10 (Spring 1957), 73–78. Pertinent to Lytle are comments on p. 76.

Hurt, James R. "Lytle's 'Jerico, Jerico, Jerico'." *Explicator*, 20 (February 1962), Item 52.

Jones, Madison. "A Look at 'Mister McGregor'." *Mississippi Quarterly*, 23 (Fall 1970), 363–370. Reprinted this collection.

Karanikas, Alexander. *Tillers of A Myth: Southern Agrarians as Social and Literary Critics*. Madison: University of Wisconsin Press, 1966. Scattered references to Lytle.

Krickel, Edward. "The Whole and the Parts: Initiation in 'The Mahogany Frame'." *Mississippi Quarterly*, 23 (Fall 1970), 391–405. Reprinted this collection.

Landess, Thomas H. "Unity of Action in *The Velvet Horn*." *Mississippi Quarterly*, 23 (Fall 1970), 349–361. Reprinted this collection.

Landman, Sidney J. "The Walls of Mortality." *Mississippi Quarterly*, 23 (Fall 1970), 415–423. Reprinted this collection.

Leisy, Earnest E., *The American Historical Novel*. Norman, Oklahoma: University of Oklahoma Press, 1950. Pp. 224 and 251 contain brief comments on Lytle.

Lively, Robert. *Fiction Fights the Civil War: An Unfinished Chapter in the Literary History of the American People*. Chapel Hill:

University of North Carolina Press, 1957. Pp. 184–186 discuss *The Long Night*. See also the index for other scattered references.

Lyell, F. H. "Larger Patterns of Life." *New York Times Book Review*, 31 August 1958, p. 6. Review of *A Novel, A Novella and Four Stories*.

Macauley, Robie. "Big Novel." *Kenyon Review*, 19 (Autumn 1957), 644–646. Reviews *The Velvet Horn*.

Marsh, F. T. "Mystery and Terror in Mr. Lytle's Novel of the South." *New York Times Book Review*, 6 September 1936, p. 9. Review of *The Long Night*.

Mencken, H. L. "Uprising in the Confederacy." *American Mercury*, 22 (March 1931), 379–381. Reviews *I'll Take My Stand*. One sentence (p. 381) concerns Lytle.

Meneely, A. Howard. "Old Forrest." *Saturday Review of Literature*, 8 (25 July 1931), 4.

Milton, George Fort. "Forrest Against Sheridan." *Virginia Quarterly Review*, 8 (January 1932), 127–132.

Moore, Edward M. "The Nineteen-Thirty Agrarians." *Sewanee Review*, 71 (Winter 1963), 133–142. Reviews the 1962 Harper Torchbook publication of *I'll Take My Stand*. Pertinent to Lytle are pp. 134, 140.

Nemerov, Howard. "The Nature of Novels." *Partisan Review*, 24 (Fall 1957), 597–607. Pp. 601–602 concern *The Velvet Horn*.

Newby, Idus A. "The Southern Ag[r]arians: A View After Thirty Years." *Agricultural History*, 37 (July 1963), 143–155. Scattered references to Lytle which attempt to place him in the context of his Fugitive/Agrarian peers.

Parks, Edd Winfield. "Six Southern Novels." *Virginia Quarterly Review*, 13 (Winter 1937), 154–160. Pertinent to Lytle is p. 157.

Peden, William. "On the Short Story Scene." *Virginia Quarterly Review*, 35 (Winter 1959), 153–160. *NN4S* review on pp. 153–155.

Phelps, Robert. "Dust for an Adam." *National Review*, 4 (24 August 1957), 162–163. Review of *The Velvet Horn*.

Polk, Noel. "Andrew Nelson Lytle: A Bibliography of His Writings." *Mississippi Quarterly*, 23 (Fall 1970), 435–491.

Pressly, Thomas J. "Agrarianism: An Autopsy." *Sewanee Review*, 49 (April–June 1941), 145–163. Lytle is discussed in several scattered references.

Ransom, John Crowe. "Fiction Harvest." *Southern Review*, 2 (Autumn 1936), 399–418. Pp. 403–405 discuss *The Long Night*.

Rock, Virginia. "Dualisms in Agrarian Thought." *Mississippi Quarterly*, 13 (Spring 1960), 80–89. Lytle is referred to on pp. 85–87.

————. "The Fugitive-Agrarians in Response to Social Change."

Southern Humanities Review, 1 (Summer 1967), 170–181. P. 174 is pertinent to Lytle.

———. "The Making and Meaning of *I'll Take My Stand:* A Study in Utopia-Conservatism, 1925–1939." Unpublished doctoral dissertation, University of Minnesota, 1961.

Rodgers, Elizabeth H. "The Quest Theme in Three Novels by Andrew Lytle." Unpublished doctoral dissertation, Emory University, 1971.

Rolo, Charles. Review of *A Novel, A Novella and Four Stories. Atlantic*, 202 (September 1958), 81–82.

Rosenberger, Coleman. Review of *A Novel, A Novella and Four Stories. Books*, 28 September 1958, p. 12.

———. Review of *The Velvet Horn. Books*, 18 August 1957, p. 3.

Rubin, Louis D., Jr. *The Curious Death of the Novel: Essays in American Literature*. Baton Rouge: LSU Press, 1967. See index for numerous scattered references to Lytle.

———. *The Faraway Country: Writers of the Modern South*. Seattle: University of Washington Press, 1963. See index for scattered references to Lytle.

———. "Introduction to the Torchbook Edition," *I'll Take My Stand: The South and the Agrarian Tradition* by Twelve Southerners. New York: Harper, 1962, pp. vi–xviii.

Rugoff, Milton. Review of *At the Moon's Inn. Books*, 30 November 1941, p. 10.

Shapiro, Edward S. "The American Distributists and the New Deal." Unpublished doctoral dissertation, Harvard University, 1968.

Stewart, John Lincoln. *The Burden of Time: The Fugitives and Agrarians*. Princeton, N.J.: Princeton University Press, 1965. Scattered references to Lytle.

Sullivan, Walter. "Southern Novelists and the Civil War." In *Southern Renascence: The Literature of the Modern South*, ed. Louis D. Rubin, Jr., and Robert D. Jacobs. Baltimore: The Johns Hopkins Press, 1953. Pp. 117–119 are concerned with *The Long Night*.

Tate, Allen. "A Prodigal Novel of Pioneer Alabama." *Books*, 6 September 1936, p. 3. Reviews *The Long Night*.

———. "Foreword" to *The Hero With the Private Parts*. Reprinted this collection as "The Local Universality of Andrew Lytle."

Terry, C. V. Review of *A Name for Evil. New York Times Book Review*, 17 August 1947, p. 17.

Thompson, C. W. "Bedford Forrest, the Confederacy's Greatest General." *New York Times Book Review*, 5 July 1931, p. 3.

Toledano, B. C. "Savannah Writers' Conference—1939." *Georgia Re-*

view, 22 (Summer 1968), 145–158. Record of a conference to which Lytle contributed.

Trowbridge, Clinton W. "The Word Made Flesh: Andrew Lytle's *The Velvet Horn*." *Critique*, 10 (1967–68), 53–68.

Ward, C. A. "The Good Myth"; "Myths: Further Vanderbilt Agrarian Views." *University of Kansas City Review*, 25 (Summer, Fall 1958), 53–56; 272–276. Pp. 55, 56 are pertinent to Lytle.

Warfel, Harry R. "Andrew Lytle." In his *American Novelists of Today*. New York: American Book Company, 1951, p. 273. Mr. Warfel quotes from what is apparently a letter from Lytle to him.

Warren, Robert Penn. "Andrew Lytle's *The Long Night*: A Rediscovery." *Southern Review*, 7 n.s. (Winter 1971), 130–139. Reprinted on pp. 18–28 of *Rediscoveries*, ed. David Madden. New York: Crown Publishers, Inc., 1971.

Weatherby, H. L. "The Quality of Richness: Observations on Andrew Lytle's *The Long Night*." *Mississippi Quarterly*, 23 (Fall 1970), 383–390. Reprinted this collection.

Weston, Robert. "Toward a Total Reading of Fiction: The Essays of Andrew Lytle." *Mississippi Quarterly*, 23 (Fall 1970), 425–433.

Wilson, Edmund. "Books—Miscellaneous Recommendations." *New Yorker*, 23 (20 September 1947), 97. Reviews *A Name for Evil*.

Yeh-Wei Yu, Frederick. "Andrew Lytle's *A Name for Evil* as a Redaction of 'The Turn of the Screw.'" *Michigan Quarterly Review*, 11 (Summer 1972), 186–190.

Index